Whole Language Units

for

Science

Written by Deborah Plona Cerbus & Cheryl

Illustrated by Cheryl Buhler, Sue Fullam, and Keith Vasc....

Teacher Created Materials, Inc.
P.O. Box 1040
Huntington Beach, CA 92647
©1993 Teacher Created Materials, Inc.
Made in U.S.A.

ISBN 1-55734-201-6

Table of Contents

Introduction

The purpose of whole language is to provide a literacy-rich environment in which children learn to use and enjoy written and spoken language naturally. The children become immersed in print and use their developing language skills in purposeful activities. In *Whole Language Units for Science*, children learn about their world aided by literature and original poetry. They will learn to enjoy and increase their proficiency in written and spoken language. With the teacher modeling oral language, the children will appreciate literature, hear rhyming patterns, and learn new concepts. Children will use thinking skills such as brainstorming and predicting, in addition to creating their own innovations.

Each unit in this book begins with a children's literature selection which relates to a science topic. In addition, each unit contains some or all of the following:

- related literature
- sample lesson plans
- riddles
- games
- creative writing
- center ideas
- brainstorming
- original poetry

- flannel-board patterns
- art projects
- songs
- reproducible little books
- phonics activities
- home/school connecting activities
- recipes
- culminating activities

Activities may be chosen to fit the needs of your classroom and your teaching style. Although each unit is designed to last approximately one week, it may be lengthened or shortened to suit any curriculum.

What Is Whole Language?

Whole language programs are based on the belief that children should learn to read and write naturally, just as they learned to speak. The goals are for the children to learn to read and write and to learn to love reading and writing.

In a whole language program, skill development and enrichment activities are arranged around a literary experience. Instead of teaching reading, language, writing, spelling, and speaking as separate units, the teacher relates all of these to a particular book, story, or poem. Students listen to a whole text and experience its meaning. This is accomplished not just by asking a few questions about the story, but by immersing the class in repeated experiences with the story. Children learn best and become involved in their learning by listening, speaking, reading, writing, drawing, and touching. When possible, students should act out or "play" the stories.

Whole language strategies involve a series of daily activities based on books. The teacher reads aloud to the children several times a day for their enjoyment, modeling enthusiasm and good reading behavior. Listening together gives the children a common background to use in extending the literature throughout the school day.

Since literature is the focus of the whole language classroom, children are given plenty of opportunities to practice reading. Children listen to stories, rhymes, and poems and are encouraged to make predictions, inferences, and deductions. They are also given time to read independently. Reading is supported with activities that combine listening, writing, speaking, and illustrating.

Writing is also an essential component of a balanced whole language program. Children use ideas or patterns from stories they have read to create new stories. Younger children need lots of direction, modeling, and suggestions from the teacher. Students use invented spelling during creative writing. They are encouraged not to worry about correct spelling, but to sound out a word and spell it the best they can. Spelling correction may intimidate very young writers. Older students can correct and edit a second draft.

A whole language classroom provides a print-rich environment. Walls and bulletin boards are covered with labeled pictures and creative writing. New words from instructional units are displayed on experience charts or on word bank posters. Copies of literature and Big Books are available in a reading center along with books written by the students. The entire classroom has a colorful and stimulating environment with specific work centers, a variety of materials for reading and writing that are changed frequently, and numerous displays of students' work and projects.

Preparing for a Whole Language Unit

Before using a whole language unit, prepare the materials necessary for teaching the unit. Some general suggestions are given below.

Gathering Materials: Go to your school or public library to locate the featured literature which relates to the theme. Look up the songs listed at the beginning of each unit. Check to see if the unit requires any props or puppets for storytelling or story keepsakes for the children to take home. Read the sample lesson plans to see if any other materials, such as sentence strips or chart paper, are required.

Sending Parent Letters: Each unit contains a parent letter. Copy it and send it home either before the unit begins or on the first day of the unit.

Using the Poetry: Make an overhead transparency of the poetry page. You might also want to print the poem on chart paper or on sentence strips. Individual copies of the poem can be kept in a poetry folder.

Making Little Books: Reproduce the pages of the little books. Books may be assembled before the lesson or students may help complete the following steps. Cut on the dotted lines. Check to make sure the pages are in the right order. Staple the pages together. Students may use crayons or markers to color their little books. They should be read together as a class; partners can take turns reading them to each other, and then they can be taken home to share with parents.

Using Activity Pages: Reproduce appropriate unit activity pages for the children. Directions for using the pages are given in the sample lesson plans for each unit.

Preparing the Games: Reproduce the game pieces on heavy paper. Color and laminate all the pieces and store them in self-sealing bags. Label each bag with the name of the game.

Using the Patterns: Patterns are provided with many of the units. Trace these patterns onto felt or Pellon 930 for use on a flannel board. Some patterns may be enlarged, traced on tagboard, and laminated for use in various center activities or on bulletin boards. The patterns can also be used to make stick puppets or story props for retelling the stories.

Setting Up Classroom Centers

Many different types of centers are appropriate in a whole language classroom. The following are general suggestions for types of centers and the materials needed in them. Refer to the "Centers" page in each unit for specific center activities.

Reading Center: Fiction and nonfiction books (including copies of featured literature), poetry books, magazines, Big Books, copies of little books, student-made books, word charts, a pocket chart, a flannel board, sentence strips, chart paper, overhead projector, comfortable chairs, pillows, and rugs.

Listening Center: Tape recorder and headphones, copies and tapes of the little books and the featured literature selections.

Writing Center: A variety of types of paper, pencils, washable markers, crayons, alphabet stamps, wooden letters, magnetic letters and board, word bank posters, pictionaries, typewriter, a computer with a simple word processing program, and blank journals and books.

Social Studies Center: A globe, maps, pictures of people from around the world, an interest table for items from other countries, picture books and informational books about people and families around the world, career hats.

Math Center: A flannel board, number stamps, wooden numbers, magnetic numbers and board, an estimating jar, pattern blocks, small cubes, tangrams, small objects for counting (such as plastic teddy bears), a floor graph, a balance scale.

Science Center: Observation journals, posters and pictures, science books (both picture books and informational texts), a science "please touch" table, plants and seeds, seed and flower catalogs, science magazines such as *Ranger Rick* and *Your Big Backyard*, and a class pet.

Art Center: White and colored paper of various sizes and textures, paints, crayons, markers, colored chalk, clay, glitter, tissue paper, old magazines, and fabric scraps and trims.

Dramatic Play Center: Child-sized furniture, kitchen area, dishes and play food, a telephone, dress-up clothes, a dollhouse, multicultural dolls, puppets, and stuffed animals, blocks of all shapes and sizes (wooden, plastic, cardboard), plastic interconnecting blocks, vehicles, traffic signs, a barn with farm animals.

Growing and Changing

Featured Literature: *Leo the Late Bloomer*

Author: Robert Kraus

Publisher: Scholastic, Inc., 1971

Summary: This book is a colorful, classic children's favorite. As Leo the tiger struggles to learn to read, write, and draw, his feelings reflect those experienced by all children as they grow up. When his family gives him the gifts of time and patience, Leo eventually blooms.

Additional Literature: *I'm Growing* by Aliki Brandenburg (Harper Collins, 1992); *When You Were a Baby* by Ann Jonas (Puffin Books, 1986); *Sometimes Things Change* by Patricia Eastman (Children's Press, 1983); *When I Get Bigger* by Mercer Mayer (Western Publishing Co., 1983). *You'll Soon Grow into Them, Titch* by Pat Hutchins (Greenwillow Books, 1983); *When I Grow Up* by Heidi Goennel (Little, Brown & Co., 1987); *Eye Openers: Baby Animals* from Eye Openers Series (Macmillan, 1992).

Related Songs: "I Am Special" by Judy Bush, *Piggyback Songs* (Warren Publishing House, 1983); "Special Me" by Kristine Wagoner, *More Piggyback Songs* (Warren Publishing House, 1984); "I Wonder If I'm Growing" by Raffi, *Raffi Singable Songbook*, (Crown, 1987); "Head and Shoulders" from *Wee Sing* by Pam Beall and Susan Nipp (Price, Stern, Sloan, 1983).

Day 1: Read the title *Leo the Late Bloomer* to the class. Does anyone know what a late bloomer is? To facilitate understanding of the phrase, discuss the flower-blooming process. Show the cover. Can the children predict which animal is Leo and what he might do in the story? Can the children guess what the animals are feeling — and why — from the expressions on their faces? Name each animal and talk about the unusual bird called a "plover." After the story, can the children explain why Leo's mother told his father to be patient? How did Leo change during the story and what new things did he learn?

Display the page where the animals write their names. Have the children practice writing their own names — an important accomplishment for young children. After learning their own names, children frequently start to identify classmates' names. Print each of the children's names on a sentence strip. Use photographs taken in class or brought from home for a game of matching names to pictures. Have children compare names. Can they find a name that's shorter, longer, the same length as their name? Can they sort names by grouping those that start, or end, with the same letter?

Have available a supply of magnetic letters for spelling names. At the reading center, include a list of baby animal names for children to spell and illustrate.

Leo Late Bloomer

Growing and Changing *(cont.)*

Day 1 *(cont.)*: Share some of your own baby items and pictures with the children. Tell the children that even you had to practice how to talk, walk, read, and do all the things you can do now.

Make a large chart with two columns labeled "When I Was a Baby" and "Now That I'm Big." Have the class brainstorm things they did when they were a baby and things they can do now. Read the "When I Was Little" poem (page 11) and the story, *When You Were A Baby*. Have the children fold a large piece of white construction paper in half; then have them paint a picture of themselves as a baby on the top section and a current picture on the bottom. Add a sentence to the baby picture, such as, "When I was little, I liked to play with my rattle;" the other picture might say, "Now that I am big, I like to play with trucks."

Begin teaching some of the songs for this unit.

As you work with this unit, take slides of the children at work in your classroom for use in the culminating activity. Also, invite the children to bring in some of their own baby items to share. Send home the parent letter found on page 10. *Body unit*

Day 2: Start out by singing "Head and Shoulders" from the *Wee Sing* song book by Pam Beall and Susan Nipp. Talk about the different body parts and how they change as we grow. Trace one of the children on a large piece of paper and cut out the body shape. Write labels for arms, legs, etc. and tape them on the outline; display in the science center.

Read *I'm Growing*, which appropriately explains how we grow and change as we get older. The book also mentions how the body needs food and exercise to grow strong and healthy. After reading the story, have an adult helper weigh and measure each child. This should be done three times during the year so comparisons can be made. Cut long strips of paper or string to represent the children's heights and arrange them in order — shortest to tallest — on a wall or bulletin board. Construct a bar graph for weight.

When the children bring in their birth lengths and weights (see Parent Letter, page 10), display the information in the same way as the current measurements.

Day 3: Discuss how, as people grow and change, they make decisions about work. Make a word web using the word "career" in the center. Ask the children to think of as many different careers (or jobs) as they can. Add all ideas to the word web, grouping the words as you write. For example, cluster all careers that involve wearing a special uniform together. Read *When I Grow Up* and add any new careers to the word web. Mention the planned writing center class book (page 9).

Growing and Changing *(cont.)*

Day 3 *(cont.)***:** Be sure children mention school careers, including that of a principal. Ask what they think principals do in their jobs. You might share the children's answers with your principal! Invite the principal to visit your class to talk about his/her job. During the visit ask the principal to read the delightful story *The Principal's New Clothes* by Stephanie Calmenson (Scholastic, 1989) which is based on the classic tale of the emperor's new clothes. If possible, take a tour of the principal's office; have your class draw pictures and write thank you notes to send after the visit.

Reread the poem for this unit and have the children make the little book. See page 4 for general directions for assembly and use.

Day 4: Collect some pictures of baby and adult animals from books or magazines or use the patterns provided on pages 19-20. Distribute pictures of the animals and ask the children to identify and pair the baby animal with the adult animal on the flannel board. Then read *Baby Animals* or one of your favorite books on this topic.

For a different perspective on growing and changing, read *Sometimes Things Change*. This book provides an opportunity for prediction with "before and after." For example, one page shows a flower and the next page shows the bud which preceded the flower. Introduce center activities. Review poem and songs learned during the week.

Day 5: Prepare for the "Look How We've Grown" open house mentioned in the parent letter. Have the children sing the songs for this unit and recite the poem, while you display the poem on the overhead with the pictures drawn by the children. Show slides of the children at work during the songs.

Make a display of the children's baby photos without their names. Have the parents guess which child goes with which picture. It's also fun to post baby pictures of school staff, so students and parents can guess their identities during an all-school open house.

Have on display many samples of the children's work: the names they practiced, the class book of careers, all charts made during the week's activities; and the flannel board pictures. Encourage the children to try some of the center activities with their parents. Parents may also want to try other materials they've heard about, such as geoboards. Have the children make a geoboard design prior to the visit. The parent's job is to take the design apart and make a new design using the same geobands.

Finally, serve refreshments, such as lemonade and finger sandwiches (peanut butter and jelly is a favorite), made by the children. Preparing the room and food for parents shows how the children are growing and changing!

Growing and Changing Centers

Reading Center: Let children practice the name activities described on page 6 in this center. Make available a selection of books about growing and changing, multiple copies of the little book, and a transparency or pocket chart version of the *When I Was Little* poem.

Writing Center: Have each child contribute a page to a *When We Grow Up* class book. After child draws a picture of an occupation the child wishes to have in the future, add a sentence, dictated or written in invented spelling, "When I grow up, I want to be a ..."

Have children practice writing their names at this center. Provide a model of each child's name, paper, and a variety of writing tools. As children master writing their names, award a special pencil.

Math Center: Birthdays are symbolic events representing growth and change; talking about them provides a perfect lead-in to math activities. Collect birthday cards which have numbers on the front. Have children find cards that represent their ages and count out the correct number of candles to match. The birthday cards could also be put in numerical order and an appropriate number of counters placed with each card. Use birthday candles, balloons, or small party favors for the unit's estimating jar.

Keep graphs and charts of unit weighing and measuring activities at this center.

Science Center: Prepare the patterns found on pages 19-20. Children name and match the before-and-after pictures. Encourage them to make statements such as, "When a puppy grows up, it becomes a dog."

Have some rapidly growing plants, such as a sweet potato or wheat, set up in this center; children can take weekly measurements and record growth information.

If any of the children have a kitten or puppy, ask the parents if the pet can visit once a week. Document its growth with photographs and by weighing and measuring it during each visit.

Dramatic Play Center: Provide baby dolls, clothing, and equipment so children can pretend to be moms and dads. Children will gain good experience by matching doll clothes by size.

Include an assortment of hats, costumes, and props to represent different careers in this center.

Have the children attempt to build a tower of blocks to match their own height or that of a classmate; have one child lie on the floor so several classmates can build a wall or a train of blocks that is just as long as the child.

Art Center: An ongoing activity is to have the children draw self portraits at the end of each month. These pictures provide a valuable record of growth and give parents a nice keepsake book at the end of the year. Pages are provided for this book on pages 16-18.

Large self portraits also make a nice display for an open house.

Parent Letter

Dear Parents,

We are just starting a new unit of science study about growth and change. The children will look back to when they were babies and discover how much they have learned to do since then. We will also study baby animals and talk about other living things that grow and change such as an acorn that grows into an oak tree. Some of our featured literature for this unit is *Leo the Late Bloomer* by Robert Kraus and *I'm Growing* by Aliki. Both stories stress the idea that we all grow and learn in our own special way and that sometimes children need the gifts of time and patience.

Our activities will cross many different subject areas: science, math, social studies, art, music, reading, and writing. Here's a preview of some of our activities:

1. Drawing monthly self portraits so we can see how we grow and change this year.

2. Talking about what we want to be when we grow up.

3. Making a little book about growing and changing that your child will enjoy reading with you at home.

One of our math activities for this unit will be to compare and graph our birth weights and lengths. Please complete the form below and send it to school by _____. Thanks for your help!

As a culminating activity for this unit we will have a special "Look How We've Grown" open house on _____. We will share with you some of the many things we are learning to do at school. We look forward to seeing you then!

Sincerely,

Please send this form back to school by _____, along with a small baby picture of your child. The baby picture will be returned to you.

Child's name: _____

Birth weight was: _____

Birth length was: _____

When I Was Little

I grow taller
With the passing days.
I'm changing daily
In many ways.

When I was little
I could only creep.
But now I run
And skip and leap.

When I was little
I drank milk so neat.
Now all kinds of foods
Are what I eat.

When I was little
I slept through the day.
Now I have fun
With friends when we play.

When I was little
I could cry or coo.
But now I can talk
Or sing to you.

When I was little
I was rocked by Mom and Dad.
But now that I'm big
Their hugs make me glad.

I grow taller
With the passing days.
I'm changing daily
In many ways.

Making Little Books

My Little Book of

When I Was Little

Name _____

I grow taller
With the passing days.
I'm changing daily
In many ways.

1

Making Little Books *(cont.)*

When I was little

I could only creep.

But now I run

And skip and leap.

2

When I was little

I drank milk so neat.

Now all kinds of foods

Are what I eat.

3

Making Little Books *(cont.)*

When I was little

I slept through the day.

Now I have fun

With friends when we play.

4

When I was little

I could cry or coo.

But now I can talk

Or sing to you.

5

Making Little Books *(cont.)*

When I was little
I was rocked by Mom and Dad.

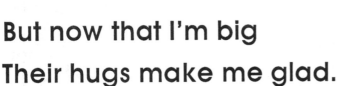

But now that I'm big
Their hugs make me glad.

6

I grow taller
With the passing days.
I'm changing daily
In many ways.

7

Monthly Self Portraits

Have the children draw a picture of themselves at the end of every month. Save the pictures, add a cover, and send the book home at the end of the year.

Monthly Self Portraits *(cont.)*

Monthly Self Portraits *(cont.)*

Patterns

Patterns *(cont.)*

20

Senses

Featured Literature: *My Five Senses*

Author: Aliki

Publisher: HarperCollins, 1989

Summary: A little boy learns all about his five senses as he investigates his world. The book gives examples of how our senses help us gather information.

Additional Literature: *Spectacles* by Ellen Raskin (Macmillan, 1968); *Here Are My Hands* by Bill Martin Jr. and John Archambault (Henry Holt and Company, Inc., 1985); *Peace at Last* by Jill Murphy (Dial Books, 1980); *The Popcorn Book* by Tomie dePaola (Holiday House, 1978); *The Five Senses*, a series of five books by Maria Rius (Barron's Educational Series, 1985); *Seeing Things, Feeling Things, Hearing Things, Smelling Things, Tasting Things* by Allan Fowler (Children's Press, 1991); *A Mouse in the House* by Henrietta (Dorling Kindersley, 1991); *The Listening Walk* by Paul Showers (HarperCollins, 1991).

Related Songs: "House Songs" by John Saltsman, "I Hear Noises" by Jean Warren, "Popcorn" by Aletha Ballengee, *More Piggyback Songs*, (Warren Publishing House, 1984).

Day 1: On the first day of this theme, bring in some items hidden in box or bag to represent each of the five senses: a chocolate bar (taste), cinnamon (smell), a bell (hearing), cotton (touch), a picture of a rainbow (sight). Show the items to the children one at a time, discussing each item's characteristics. Can the children predict the topic for the day? Can the children name the five senses? List the five senses on a piece of chart paper and draw a picture next to each word (eyes, hands, etc.).

Introduce the featured literature; discuss the cover. Can the children predict what the boy will do in the story? Read the story, stopping to ask the children if they would enjoy the boy's activities.

Introduce the "I Hear Noises" song and sing it several times. Teach and review other songs throughout the week. Present "The Five Senses" poem using an overhead transparency or chart. Encourage the children to join in on a second reading and to act out the poem. Send home the parent letter found on page 25.

Day 2: Talk about the sense of sight today. Show and discuss a diagram of the eye. Have children look around the classroom and name things they like seeing and explain why.

Take children outdoors to watch cloud shapes. Can they see pictures in the clouds? Back in the classroom, make some simple cloud pictures. Fold a piece of blue construction paper in half, open the paper and randomly squirt white tempera paint on one half of the paper. Then carefully fold the paper and rub gently. When the paper is unfolded, you will have a symmetrical design. Help children write a sentence telling what they see in their "clouds."

Senses *(cont.)*

Day 2 *(cont.)*: Read *A Mouse in the House* and challenge the children to "see" and count the mice in each photograph of the book.

For today's story, read *Spectacles*, which tells of a little girl who sees things in strange ways, until she gets the eyeglasses she needs. Do the children know what "spectacles" means? After reading the story, have the children experiment with vision by looking through various materials such as waxed paper, plastic wrap (both clear and colored), scraps of laminating film, and magnifying glasses. Color lenses are also commercially available. Have some fun with 3-D glasses by making a cardboard frame with red cellophane in the right lens and green cellophane in the left lens. If the children use only red and green to draw, their picture will look 3-D when the children wear the glasses. Display magnifying and various colored lenses in the Science Center for children's experimentation.

Follow up today's lesson by reading the factual book, *Seeing Things*. This book, one of the series on the senses, is a photo essay on the sense of sight. Discuss what it means to be sight-impaired or blind. If possible, have a guest speaker come in with a guide dog to explain how these animals are specially trained to help blind people. Share a sample of Braille with the class; discuss. Ask the district consultant to produce a guest speaker or helpful resource materials that will teach the children about sight-impaired people.

Day 3: Reread "The Five Senses" poem and have the children color, cut, and assemble the little book. Then gather a collection of different textured items; sit in a circle and have the children take turns reaching into a bag to touch one of the items. Can each child describe how the item feels? What might the item be? Then read *Feeling Things* and talk about some words used to discuss touch: soft, hard, rough, smooth, wet, and dry. Can the class categorize any of the items in the collection?

Read *Here Are My Hands*. The book describes different parts of the body and explains their function. After reading the book, create a class book about hands or feet. Ask some parents to come in to help the children make handprints and footprints on sheets of construction paper. Mix tempera paint with a small amount of dishwashing soap; pour in a shallow container. Then have children dip in their hand/foot (you may need to spread the paint more evenly using a paint brush); press the hand or foot on the paper to create the print. Include a caption, such as "These are Christopher's hands," and assemble into a class book. Have children brainstorm what hands and feet do; write ideas on sentence strips and place with the prints in your display.

Have children finger paint and have them experiment with other substances, such as chocolate pudding and laundry soap flakes mixed with a little water.

Senses *(cont.)*

Day 4: Begin by asking the children to sit very quietly for about thirty seconds. Then ask them what sounds they heard; list on the chalkboard or a large piece of chart paper. Were the sounds loud or soft? Can they add to the list of sounds? Play a tape of some common sounds and try to identify each one.

The story *The Listening Walk* is available on tape. A narrator tells the story and sound effects are added. Present the story to the children in a large group, then make the tape available in the listening center.

As a follow-up to the story, take your own listening walk. Try an inside and an outside walk; when you return, have the children "draw" the sounds they heard.

Make a list of the inside and outside sounds as a Venn diagram (two circles linked together). The linked area of the circle provides a place to list sounds heard both indoors and outdoors.

Ask the music teacher to provide activities involving sound: loud and soft, high and low, rhythms. Invite band or orchestra members to perform on various instruments. If available, use a keyboard to manufacture different sounds and rhythms.

Play different styles of music: jazz, rock, classical, ethnic. Let the children move to the selections of music and discuss whether the music is fast or slow. Keep various cassette tapes and musical instruments available in the music center.

Share with the children the factual information found in the book *Hearing Things*. Talk about what it means to be hearing-impaired or deaf. This would be a good time to teach the children some simple sign language. Contact your school's consultant to the hearing-impaired for more information and assistance.

Day 5: Read *Tasting Things* and *Smelling Things* to the class. Prepare sniffing jars so children can guess some smells. Some things to include are coffee, cinnamon, peppermint extract and lemon extract (on a cotton ball), perfume, cocoa. Cover the jars so children cannot see the items. Baby food jars covered with contact paper work well. Have pictures of the items available for matching to the jars.

Have a tasting party and include some foods which are sweet, sour, bitter, and salty. Discuss how various parts of the tongue recognize the different tastes. (See *The Senses* books by Rius for a tongue "map.") Bring in some foods which the children are unfamiliar with, such as exotic fruits and vegetables.

As a culminating activity, pop popcorn (preferably in a see-through popper) and describe how it looks, sounds, and smells while popping. Make a class graph about popcorn preferences using the graphing activity found on pages 35-36. Finally, have the children munch their popcorn snack while you read *The Popcorn Book* by Tomie dePaola. Teach the popcorn song listed at the beginning of this section.

Senses Centers

Reading Center: Have literature about senses available. Make copies of the little book and the poem so children can practice: record, use a transparency, and put on sentence strips. Prepare pictures of the sense organs (page 31) for the flannel board and put up as the poem is recited.

Make sandpaper letters; children trace letters with their fingers or make "rubbings." (Do likewise with numbers in the math center.)

Writing Center: Have each child make a mini-book about the senses.

Make large class books in the shape of a sense organ for each sense. Add sentences and illustrations. For example: touch — glue in tactile items and insert caption ("Feathers feel soft"/"Sandpaper feels rough.")

Have children make lists of things they like to taste, see, etc.

Math Center: Find five jars of the same size to make estimating jars for the five senses. The contents of each jar will represent one of the senses: small pretzels (taste), marbles (hearing), different colored cubes (sight), cotton balls (touch), and cinnamon sticks (smell). Have paper available by each jar so children can write down their estimates. At the end of the unit, count the objects in each jar to find out the actual amounts.

Play a counting match game using the sense of touch. The children work in pairs and sit facing their partner. Behind each child place a small pile of counting cubes; in front, place a stack of number cards. One child draws a number and says what it is and the other child then builds a unifix train with that number of cubes. Since the trains are built behind the children's backs they have to rely on their sense of touch to count out the correct number of cubes.

Finally, use sandpaper numbers as described for letters in the reading center. Both letters and numbers can be traced in sand or salt for a tactile experience.

House Center: Set up a grocery store or restaurant in your house area. Children can write lists of favorite foods as mentioned in the writing center activities. Sort empty food containers by taste (sweet, sour, bitter, salty) or by other criteria (food I dislike/like).

Art Center: Obtain some prints of varied types of artwork from your local library. Explain to the children the phrase "beauty is in the eye of the beholder." Have them paint or draw in one of the styles they consider beautiful.

Create textured collages with a variety of materials: yarn, cotton, sandpaper, lace, etc.

Block Center: Gather a collection of blocks of different shapes. Put the blocks in a bag or container so they are hidden. Each child reaches into the bag, feels a shape, and guesses what the shape is. Play the same game with pattern blocks.

Parent Letter

Dear Parents,

In our new science unit, we will learn about our five senses: sight, hearing, taste, touch, and smell. Our featured literature for this unit is *The Five Senses* by Aliki. In this story, a boy learns about his senses as he explores his world. We will also use a series of books by Maria Rius titled *The Five Senses*.

As we learn through whole-group participation and tasks at our classroom centers, our activities will extend across many different areas: reading, writing, math, poetry, art, and music. Your child will bring home a little book about the senses to read with you and share some of what we learned at school.

Some of our activities will include:
1. Finger painting with different textures for our sense of touch.
2. Holding a tasting party and discovering whether foods are sweet, sour, bitter, or salty.
3. Learning about the sight- or hearing-impaired and special tools that they use.
4. Learning how our senses work.
5. Taking a listening walk, then writing or drawing about what we've heard.

You can do many activities at home to increase your child's understanding of the five senses.

Taste: Ask your child to describe if the food he/she is eating tastes sweet, sour, bitter, or salty. Encourage your child to take a "no thank you" bite of new foods (they take one bite and if they don't like the food, they simply say, "No, thank you").

Sight: Look at fluffy clouds on a nice day and use your imagination to see pictures. Also, try some of the many books available now in which children have to find a hidden character or picture.

Smell: As you are cooking, encourage your child to sniff and guess what is in the oven. Have your child help with the cooking and experience pleasant smells such as cinnamon, and strong smells such as onion!

Hearing: Play a follow-the-directions game. Challenge your child to follow one, two, and three-step directions.

Touch: Fill a bag or a box with items that have different textures (sandpaper, a toothbrush, cotton, wax paper, etc.) Have your child reach in the bag without looking, feel one item, describe how it feels (hard, soft, rough, smooth) and try to guess what it is.

Thank you for increasing your child's learning by participating in these at-home activities.

Sincerely,

The Five Senses

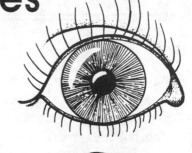

All my five senses help me know

About the world in which I grow.

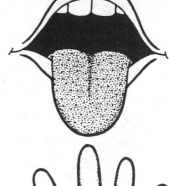

I use my eyes, so I can see

The sky, the clouds, a bird, a bee.

My little tongue tastes what I eat —

Does it taste sour? Salty? Sweet?

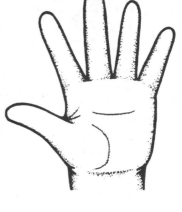

I need my fingers very much.

I need them for my sense of touch.

Day in, day out I use my nose.

Do I smell pickles? Or is it a rose?

With my ears, I clearly hear

All kinds of sounds — both far and near.

All my five senses help me know

About the world in which I grow.

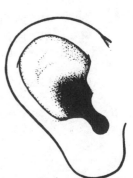

Making Little Books

- -

My Little Book of
The Five Senses

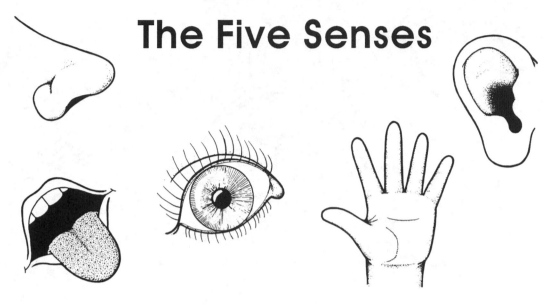

Name_____

- -

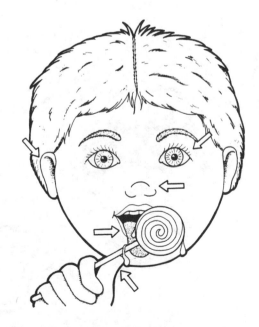

All my five senses help me know
About the world in which I grow.

1

Making Little Books *(cont.)*

I use my eyes, so I can see
The sky, the clouds, a bird, a bee.

2

My little tongue tastes what I eat —
Does it taste sour? Salty? Sweet?

3

28

Making Little Books *(cont.)*

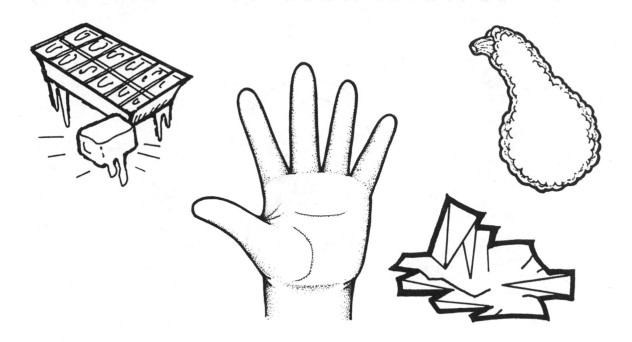

I need my fingers very much.

I need them for my sense of touch.

4

Day in, day out I use my nose.

Do I smell pickles? Or is it a rose?

5

Making Little Books *(cont.)*

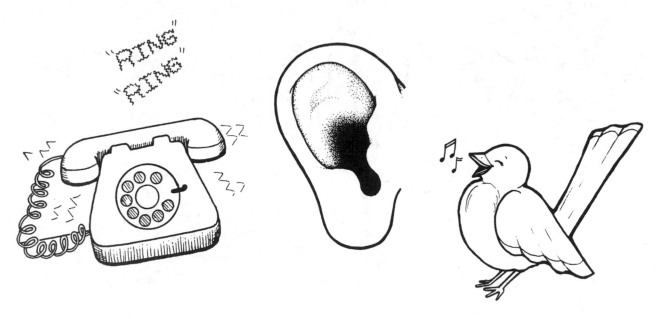

With my ears, I clearly hear

All kinds of sounds — both far and near.

6

All my five senses help me know

About the world in which I grow.

7

Patterns

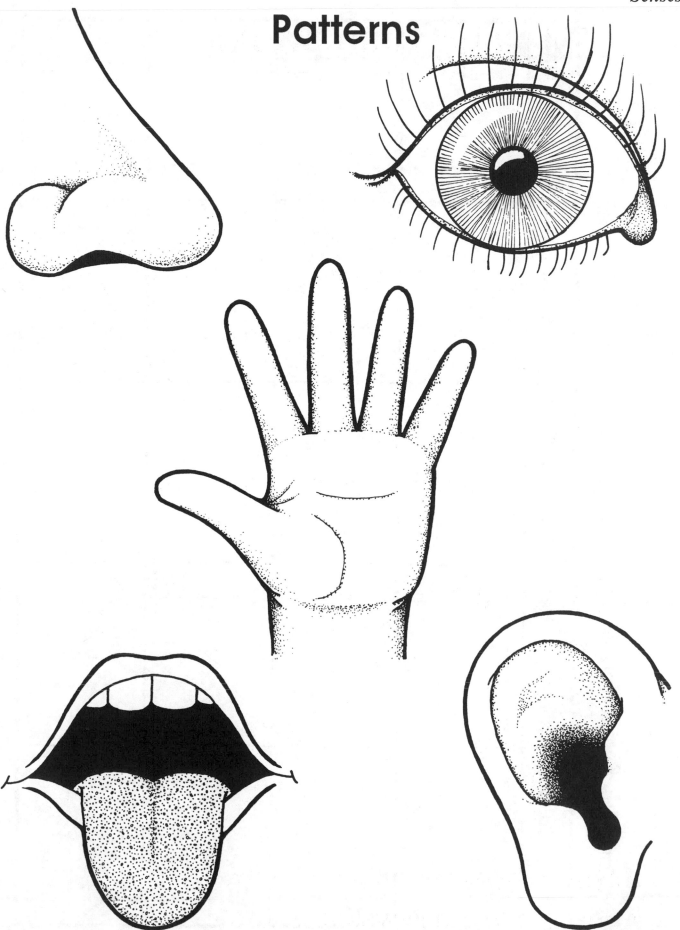

My Senses Chart

Color and cut out the pictures on page 33. Glue them in the correct column.

Things I Can See	Things I Can Hear	Things I Can Taste	Things I Can Feel	Things I Can Smell

Pictures For My Senses Chart

See directions on page 32.

Mini-book of Senses

My Mini-book of Senses

I like to touch _____ .

I like to hear _____ .

I like to smell _____ .

I like to see _____ .

I like to taste _____ .

34

Popcorn Graph

Enlarge and use these signs to create a picture graph on a bulletin board. For a description of the activity see page 23.

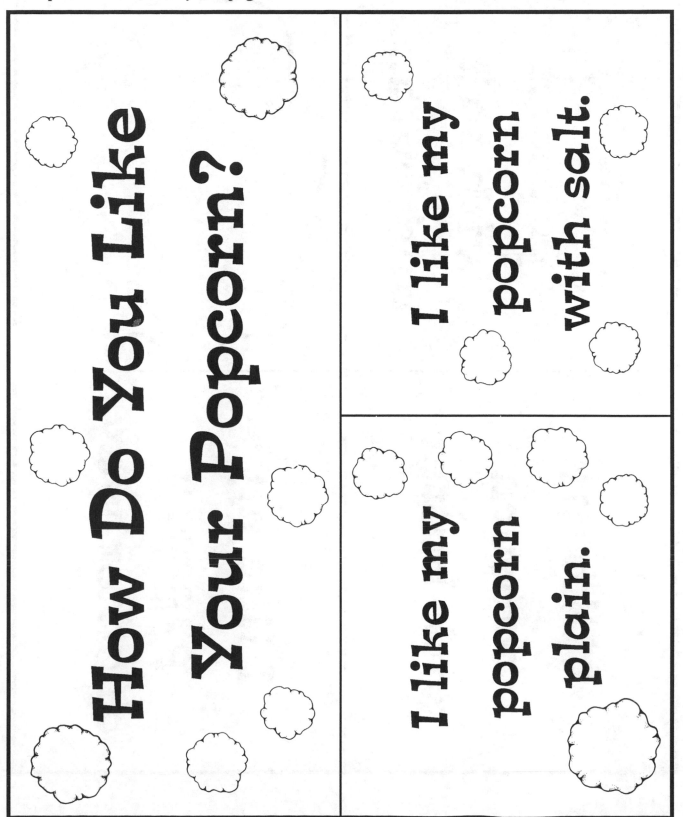

Popcorn Graph *(cont.)*

I like my popcorn with salt and butter.

I like my popcorn with butter.

I like my popcorn another way.

Pets

Featured Literature: *Hugo at the Window*

Author: Anne Rockwell

Publisher: Macmillan, 1988

Summary: A little dog named Hugo waits and watches patiently at the window for his master to return. The story follows Hugo's friend as he goes from store to store on a busy street. At the end of the story, a surprise is revealed to Hugo. His friend has bought cupcakes, a red doggie sweater, and a bone — all in preparation for Hugo's birthday party.

Additional Literature: *Pets* (Dorling Kindersley, 1991); *Let's Get A Pet* by Rose Greydanus (Troll Associates, 1988); *The Cake That Mack Ate* by Rose Robart (The Atlantic Monthly Press, 1986); *The Little Kitten* by Judy Dunn (Random House, 1983); *The Little Puppy* by Judy Dunn (Random House, 1984); *Cookie's Week* by Cindy Ward (Scholastic. Inc., 1988); *What Would You Do with a Bone?* by Barney Saltzberg (Barron's, 1986); *Good Dog, Carl* by Alexandra Day (Scholastic, 1985); *See How They Grow: Puppy* by Jane Burton (Dorling Kindersley, 1991); *Clifford's Birthday Party* by Norman Bridwell (Scholastic, 1991).

Related Songs: "How Much Is That Doggie in the Window?" from *Sharon, Lois, & Bram's Great Big Hits* (Elephant Records, 1992); "Bingo" from *Wee Sing* by Pamela Cohn Beall and Susan Hagen Nipp (Price, Stern, Sloan, 1979); "I Have a Dog" and "Three Little Puppy Dogs" by Carla K. Skjong, "I'm a Little Cat" by Betty Silkunas, "I Know a Cat" by Susan M. Paprocki, "I'm a Little Fishy" by Lynn Beaird, *Animal Piggyback Songs* by Jean Warren (Warren Publishing House, 1990).

Day 1: Display stuffed animal pets, along with a variety of books about pets, to create interest when beginning this theme. Read the title of the featured book to the children and ask them to predict what the story might be about. List the predictions on a large piece of chart paper. Then show the cover of the book and ask for additional predictions. Now, what do you think the story is about? Who is Hugo? Why do you think he's at the window? Who is the man in the green hat? What do you think will happen in this story?

This is an excellent book for talking about the importance of picture clues, since the children have to determine, based on the illustrations, what Hugo's friend is planning. Also, ask if the children see anything repeated in each picture. If they look closely, they will find a cat and a bird in different locations on many of the pages. As you read, check to see if any of the predictions came true and see if the children can guess the surprise ending of the story. When you get to the last page which shows the birthday party, have the class sing, "Happy Birthday" to Hugo.

Pets *(cont.)*

Day 1 *(cont.)*: As a follow-up to the story, brainstorm a list of animals which can be pets. Enlarge and laminate the dog or cat shape found on page 52, or the pet store shape on page 48; write the list on it with a wipe-off pen. As you write the list, talk about what letters each of the pet names starts with and ask the children if any of the names start with the same letters. Finally, have each child draw a picture of a birthday present for Hugo. Cut some pieces of birthday wrapping paper the same size as the drawing paper and staple it to the top of the present. Add a real bow to complete the effect. Children lift the flaps to reveal their present for Hugo.

Send home the parent letter found on page 42.

Day 2: Read the poem about pets as a warm-up for today's story which is an informational book. This is a good opportunity to point out the difference between expository or informational text and a narrative or story. Read *Pets*, which gives facts about many different kinds of pets: a dog, parakeet, cat, guinea pig, rabbit, goldfish, hamster, and turtle. After the story, divide the class into small cooperative groups. Have each group choose one of the animals; paint it and label its parts.

Another excellent informational book is *See How They Grow: Puppy*, one of a series of books showing how animals grow. This photo-essay book details the life of a puppy from one day old to eight weeks old.

Reread *Hugo* and draw attention to more details in the illustrations. The action in each of the windows depicted in the street scene tells a story. For example, one window shows some people going through the various steps needed to paint a room. In the bakery window, cupcakes are being sold, and this scene provides a good opportunity to present some verbal subtraction problems. Another detail to point out is the signs on the stores. Ask the children if they recognize any of the words on the signs.

Wrap up today's reading time by singing the classic song "How Much Is That Doggie in the Window?" Then change the words to include various pets; for example "How much is that rabbit in the window?" Change the second part of the song to describe the animal's tail (such as "puffy tail" for the rabbit). Have the children help with the innovation of the song and write the new words on sentence strips for use in a pocket chart.

Day 3: Reread the "Pet Shop" poem; have children color, cut, and assemble the little book of the poem. Read the little book several times each day before sending it home on the last day of this thematic unit.

Day 3 (cont.): Enlarge the dog and cat shapes found on page 52 on tagboard; write the captions, "What I Know About Dogs" and "What I Know About Cats." Laminate the shapes and, using a wipe-off marker, list the facts the children know about cats and dogs. Read *The Little Kitten* and *The Little Puppy* to learn more about cats and dogs. Then read *Cookie's Week*, a delightful story about a cat's daily routine during a week. Write sentences from the story on sentence strips for use in the pocket chart. Write the days of the week in a different color to draw attention to them.

Point to one of the days of the week and have one of the children find the word on your classroom calendar. At the end of the story, have the children predict some other things Cookie might do the next week. Make the children's ideas into a new Cookie story and assemble into a class book for the reading center.

In your weekly newsletter, ask parents if they have a pet to send to school for a visit. Have the children take turns observing the visiting pet and have them draw or write what they experience in their science journals (page 144). Encourage them to watch closely and notice anything they hear or see. For a class field trip, schedule a visit to a veterinarian's office. Take pictures during your trip so children can dictate a story and make it into a class photo essay book.

Day 4: Introduce the learning centers which go with this theme. Remind the class about the Hugo story and ask them to name other "famous" dogs from books, television, or movies. Read some of the *Good Dog, Carl* books. These are wordless and the children can write their own stories to go with the pictures. Read *Clifford's Birthday Party* and compare it to *Hugo at the Window*. How are the parties the same or different? Did the dogs receive the same presents? What would you give Clifford as a birthday present?

Have the children make the Pet Shop activity found on pages 48 and 49. Use these props while singing the innovations to "How Much Is That Doggie In The Window?"

Day 5: As a culminating activity for *Pets*, plan a pet parade or pet party. If you invite real pets to visit school, you'll need a large outdoor area and a parent with each pet to keep the animals separated. Or, pets may visit one at a time during show and tell.

As an alternative, have a stuffed pet parade. Each child may bring a favorite stuffed pet to school and tell a few facts about the real animal it represents. Have the children weigh and measure their pets and try sorting and classifying the pets in a variety of ways (color, size, etc.). Serve some bone-shaped sugar cookies to complete your theme on pets.

Pet Centers

Reading Center: The reading center should contain all of the literature used in this theme, along with other books about pets. Include some informational books for children who are interested in looking up some facts on a specific pet. Make available a transparency of the poem for independent practice, as well as multiple copies of the little book of *The Pet Shop*. Post the lists of *What We Know About Cats and Dogs*, and the labeled posters of the animals, made during the week.

Put word cards in your pocket chart showing the spelling for "cat," "cats," "dog," "dogs," and other pet names. Use the pictures found on pages 49-50 for children to match to the words. Have available some paper, ink pads, markers or pencils, and rubber stamps of pets. Children can stamp their pictures of pets on a piece of paper and write the appropriate word beneath the picture.

Writing Center: Have the children work at this center to create a class book about pets. Provide a model for the sentence "A _____ is a pet." Children write the sentence at the bottom of their paper and fill in the blank with the name of a favorite pet. Then illustrate using paints, markers, or crayons.

Create a dog shape and a cat shape book. Enlarge the pictures on page 52 to make covers for the class books. Have the class think of a catchy title such as "Dandy Dogs" and "Clever Cats." Record facts learned about dogs and cats or make it a book with pictures of different types of dogs and cats (spotted dogs, big dogs, striped cats, fat cats).

Math Center: Put an assortment of dog and cat items in the math center: toys, food boxes, pictures, other pet supplies. Label and laminate large pictures of a dog and cat. Have the children sort the items according to whether a dog or a cat would use it.

Fill a large jar with dog biscuits for estimating and counting. After the children predict how many biscuits are in the jar, group the biscuits by tens and ones to confirm the actual amount. Fill several jars with different sizes of biscuits to provide some variety.

The poem for this unit is useful for working with numbers, number words, and beginning subtraction. Discuss how each animal group contains one less animal. Use corresponding shapes on page 52 for counting, adding, subtracting, etc. Practice on the flannel board.

Pet Centers *(cont.)*

Have your class create a picture graph about pets to find out which pet is the class favorite. Divide a bulletin board near the math center into columns. Label each column with a labeled picture of a pet. Provide children with squares of paper on which to draw their vote for the favorite pet. After the graph is completed, children independently count the number of pets in each column and decide which pet has the most and the least number of votes. Make another graph using the information requested in the parent letter (see page 42).

Science Center: Have many different real pets in your science area for the children to take care of and observe. Some good classroom pets are fish, guinea pigs, hamsters, and rabbits. Use the science journal found on page 144 to record observations about the pets. Encourage children to write or draw everything they see and hear while watching the pets.

House Center: The house center can become a pet shop or a veterinarian office to go with this theme. To create a pet shop, collect some stuffed animals to display on shelves along with a variety of pet supplies such as collars, food, bowls, etc. Provide paper for the children to make price tags, as well as play or real money and a cash register to make sales.

A veterinarian's office needs stuffed animals, a doctor's white coat, a stethoscope, and books about pet care. If your class has visited a vet's office, they will have other ideas about how to change the house center to look like the office they visited.

Art Center: Stock the art center with many different photographs of pets. Provide materials so the children can draw or paint pictures of pets. Create some paper dogs with construction paper and attach a small piece of rolled up newspaper in their mouths. Simply create cat faces out of paper plates; print faces, and then add details with construction paper.

Put out tapes or records containing pet songs for the children to listen to. Some possibilities are listed at the beginning of this section. Children can use their pet shop windows (page 48) to act out their new versions of "How Much Is That Doggie in the Window?"

Parent Letter

Dear Parents,

Our new science unit is all about pets. We will learn about many different kinds of pets, such as dogs, cats, rabbits, and turtles. Our featured literature for this theme is *Hugo at the Window* by Anne Rockwell — a wonderful story about a dog named Hugo and his surprise birthday party. Your child will make a little book entitled *The Pet Shop* to read with you. Our planned activities include many different curriculum areas, such as reading, math, writing, art, science, and social studies. We will be:

1. Estimating the number of dog biscuits in a jar in our math center.

2. Observing a real pet and recording what we see in our science journals.

3. Reading factual books about pets, such as *The Little Kitten* and *The Little Puppy* by Judy Dunn.

We would like to make a graph showing the types of pets we have at home. Please complete the pet census sheet below and return it to school by _____. We look forward to learning all about our favorite pets.

Sincerely,

OUR PET CENSUS   Name: _____

Please write how many of each pet you have at your house. Return this census to school by _____. Thanks for your help!

dogs _____	**fish** _____	**birds** _____
cats _____	**guinea pigs** ____	**other pets**
rabbits _____	**hamsters** _____	_____
turtles _____	**snakes** _____	_____

The Pet Shop

Down at the pet shop

What do I see?

Six terrific turtles,

Will they come home with me?

Five perky parakeets,

Will they come home with me?

Four happy hamsters,

Will they come home with me?

Three ready rabbits,

Will they come home with me?

Two clever kittens,

Will they come home with me?

One spotted puppy —

Now that's the pet for me!

Making Little Books

My Little Book of

The Pet Shop

Name _____

Down at the pet shop

What do I see?

1

Making Little Books *(cont.)*

Six terrific turtles,

Will they come home with me?

2

Five perky parakeets,

Will they come home with me?

3

Making Little Books *(cont.)*

Four happy hamsters,

Will they come home with me?

4

Three ready rabbits,

Will they come home with me?

5

Making Little Books *(cont.)*

- -

Two clever kittens,

Will they come home with me?

6

- -

One spotted puppy —

Now that's the pet for me!

7

- -

Pets

My Pet Shop

Color the pet shop and animals. Cut along dotted lines. Attach the animals to wooden sticks with glue. The pets can then pop up in the pet store window.

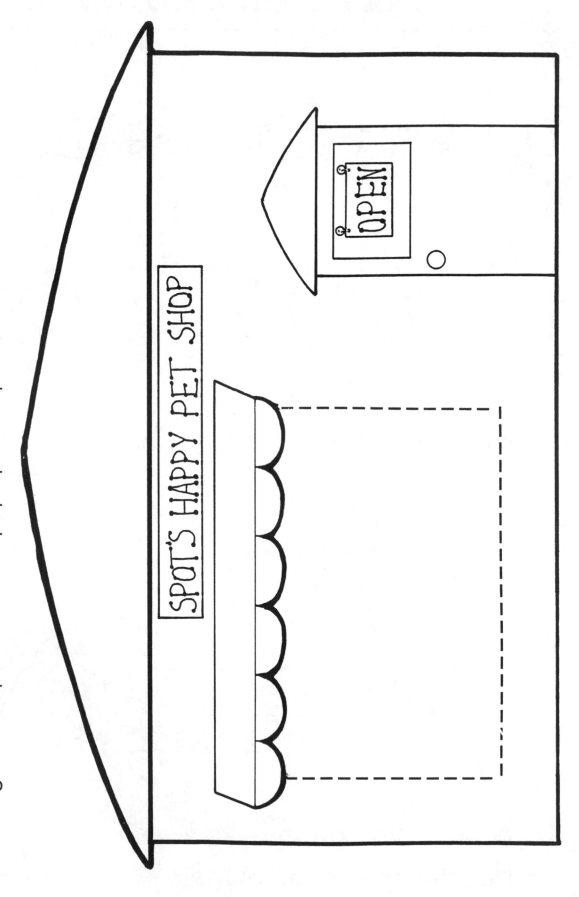

SPOT'S HAPPY PET SHOP

OPEN

48

Pet Shop Animals

See directions on page 48.

Pet Shop Animals *(cont.)*

50

Pet Riddles

Use these riddles with the patterns on page 52.

Get out the leash
We'll go for a run,
I'll bark and play.
We'll have lots of fun.
What am I?

I like it when
You stroke my fur.
Scratch my ears
And hear me purr.
What am I?

My hiding place
Is in my shell —
I live in a pond
And swim very well.
What am I?

I swish my tail,
To move very fast
And wave my fins
As I swim past.
What am I?

I'm soft and I'm cuddly
My tail puffs like cotton.
When I see you coming
I'll turn and start hopping.
What am I?

Pet Patterns

Weather

Featured Literature: *What Will the Weather Be Like Today?*

Author: Paul Rogers

Publisher: Greenwillow, 1989

Summary: Through clever verse and bright illustrations, this book gives a glimpse into the many types of weather found around the world.

Additional Literature: *What Makes the Weather* by Janet Palazzo (Troll, 1982); *Weather Words and What They Mean* by Gail Gibbons (Holiday House, 1990); *Rain* by David Bennett (Bantam Books, 1988); *Rain* by Peter Spier (Doubleday, 1982); *The Snowy Day* by Ezra Jack Keats (Viking, 1962); *Cloudy with a Chance of Meatballs* (Atheneum, 1978); *The Wind Blew* by Pat Hutchins (Scholastic, 1974); *The Cloud Book* by Tomie dePaola (Holiday House, 1975); *What's the Weather Today?* by Allan Fowler (Children's Press, 1991).

Related Songs: "Weather Song" by Sister Linda Kaman, *More Piggyback Songs* (Warren Publishing House, 1984); "The Wind" by Roberta Mohr, "Snowflakes" by Jean Warren, and "It Is Raining" by Susan Widdifield, *Piggyback Songs* (Warren Publishing House, 1983).

Day 1: Before reading the featured literature selection, make a list on chart paper of types of weather your class knows about. Include this list on your science center "Weather Wall."

As you read *What Will the Weather Be Like Today?*, introduce the classroom globe. Point out that different parts of the earth have different climates and weather due to their proximity to the equator and polar regions. Challenge your students to explain why the author says that fish wouldn't notice a change in the weather and that a mole wouldn't know if it were raining. Encourage students to find clues about unfamiliar terms in the illustrations.

Discuss the weather of the day. Take your class out-of-doors, if possible. Use page 63 to create a "Weather Observation Chart" on which to record the daily weather during this unit. (Have students record each type of weather that occurs during a day, so they will learn how quickly weather can change.) Add this chart to your science center's "Weather Wall." Introduce a new weather word every day. Write your "Weather Words of the Day" on 5" x 8" (13 cm x 20 cm) index cards, adding an illustration that gives a clue as to the meaning of the words. Start with the word "tornado" and introduce the tornado tube in your science center.

Tornado

Weather *(cont.)*

Set up a thermometer to take the temperature outside your school. Graph daily temperatures. Add the graph to your Weather Wall.

Present the "Weather" poem to your class using an overhead transparency or chart. Have students identify types of weather mentioned in the poem. Reproduce the weather shapes on pages 64 and 65; color them; and attach each to a tongue depressor. During the rereading of the poem, give these shapes to individual children to hold up at the appropriate time in the poem.

Send home the Parent Letter on page 57.

Day 2: Reread *What Will the Weather Be Like Today?* Encourage children to join in. Since the text is written in verse, emphasize the first rhyming word; have children say the second rhyming word using rhyming and context clues (say...today, hot...not, etc.)

After reading the book a few times, pull some words from the text to use as the basis for building word families. Word bases from the text include: -ot (hot, not, etc.); -og (frog, log, etc.); -ay (say, today, play, day, etc.). Write one word base at a time at the top of a strip of paper. Encourage children to think of words for a list (from the book or others) that rhyme with the given word. Give lots of examples to get them started. Read through the list several times with your students, encouraging them to take over the leadership of the reading. Display these word family lists in your reading center.

Reread the poem "Weather" using the weather shapes on tongue depressors. Allow individual students to make their own storytelling props to use in rereading the poem at school and to take home as props to use with the little books of the poem.

Day 3: If your students live in an area where they have not had contact with snow, read a book about snow, such as *The Snowy Day*, to your class. Have students observe ice cubes and explain how snow feels as cold as ice, but it falls in fluffy flakes from the sky. (You might bring in soap flakes for children to feel the lightness of flakes.) Discuss the complications that can arise when too much snow falls at one time and becomes a blizzard.

Do your Weather Observation Chart and Temperature Graph on your Weather Wall. Introduce the Weather Word of the Day: blizzard. Write the word "blizzard" on a 5" x 8" (13 cm x 20 cm) card, along with a drawing of big snowdrifts and more snowflakes falling. Include this card on your Weather Wall.

Introduce other literature about weather to your students today. *What Makes the Weather?* is a good expository text for young children. It explains different types of weather by looking at the sky. Using Peter Spier's *Rain*, a wordless book, have students tell the story shown by the illustrations of a rainy day. Use *Weather Words and What They Mean* to motivate students to suggest additional words they would like to include as "Weather Words of the Day."

Weather *(cont.)*

Read the poem "Weather" with your students. Let each child make a little book of the poem by reproducing pages 59-62 for each child. Assemble and use the books as explained on page 4.

Brainstorm lists of things to do for fun on a rainy day, a snowy day, and a sunny day. Have each child choose one type of day (rainy, snowy, or sunny), and write or dictate a sentence telling what he or she would do for fun on that kind of day. Then have children illustrate that idea. Assemble these into a class book for the reading center.

Day 4: Plan to explore wind today. Read the humorous book, *The Wind Blew*, to your class. Then go outside to observe the wind. Give each child a pinwheel (see page 66 for a pattern) or a crepe-paper streamer to use to see what the wind does.

Back inside the classroom, read David Bennett's *Rain* to your class. Then conduct an experiment to make it rain inside your classroom. Fill a teakettle about two-thirds full with water and place on a hot plate. Hold a metal cake pan (9" x 13"/23 cm x 33 cm) filled with ice cubes over the spout. As the water in the teakettle boils and the steam begins to come out of the spout, condensation will form on the bottom on the pan. When enough condensation collects, it will "rain." Try to have a plant sitting next to the hot plate so the rain will fall on the plant. Children may record their observations of this experiment in a Science Journal (see page 144).

Now that your students have a greater understanding of weather, read the classic, fictional story *Cloudy With a Chance of Meatballs*. Then have each child write and illustrate an imaginative sentence beginning with, "In my town, it would rain..." Add these to your Weather Wall.

Do your Weather Observation Chart and Temperature Graph on the Weather Wall. Add the word "rainbow" as your Weather Word of the Day. Extend the literature selections into your classroom centers. See page 56.

Day 5: If possible, celebrate the culmination of your weather unit by inviting a weather forecaster or meteorologist to visit your classroom. Otherwise, plan to present a short program for another classroom to share what you learned about weather. Have children use their storytelling props to perform the poem, sing the suggested weather songs, read the Weather Wall, show their imaginative rain pictures, share their class book, and tell what they have learned about weather.

Have children make Weather Headbands to wear during your culminating activity. Each child will need a strip of construction paper 24" x 2" (60 cm x 5 cm) for the headband. Children glue on cotton for clouds, glitter on white paper snowflakes, and blue raindrops. Children can draw a yellow sun wearing sunglasses. Encourage children to use their creativity to show what they know about weather and celebrate their learning.

Children may want to continue their Weather Observation Chart and Temperature Graph for an additional period of time. If you choose to do this, have your students notice any changes that may be seasonal in your area.

Weather Centers

Reading Center: Display copies of the unit's literature selections and the class book. Let children use the books and a copy of the poem independently, with a partner, or with a group. Have children practice the rhyming words which they have worked on with you.

Writing Center: Provide a simple format on a poster for the children to follow to write their own weather forecasts:

> _____'s Forecast for the _____ Area
>
> The forecast for today, _____, is for _____. Later in the day it will _____.
> The expected temperature is _____ degrees. Wear your _____ as you leave for school.

Children can practice presenting their forecasts at the Dramatic Play Center with a cardboard box television set.

Math Center: Reproduce pages 64-65 for children to use to create their own weather patterns. Inexpensive, colorful, little paper umbrellas to use in your estimating jar may be ordered from Oriental Trading Company, P.O. Box 3407, Omaha, NE, 68103, Phone (402) 331-5511.

Science Center: Using large block letters or a computer program, make a banner for your science center, "The Weather Wall." Have children decorate the banner with weather symbols. Place your Weather Observation Chart, Temperature Graph, Weather Words of the Day, and *Cloudy With a Chance of Meatballs* pictures here, along with all of the weather maps and articles from the newspaper you suggest children bring in. Encourage children to read the Weather Wall every day.

Have a "tornado tube," two plastic soda bottles joined by a small connector, available for your students to use. The connectors are available from Burnham Associates, Inc., Salem, MA 01970 (Item No. 220). By following the very simple directions, a simulated "tornado in a bottle" can be created for students to observe.

Social Studies Center: Have a globe available for your students to use in locating which parts of the earth are near the equator and have hot, steamy weather and which parts of the earth are near the poles and have very cold weather.

Dramatic Play Center: Have a variety of clothing items for children to use in learning to dress for the weather, such as sunglasses, umbrellas, raincoats, winter jackets, boots, and sweaters. Children can read their forecasts on a television set made from a cardboard box, while other students dress appropriately.

Art Center: Paint bright yellow suns wearing sunglasses. Make paper kites with tails to hang in your room. Do a crayon-resist snowy day picture by drawing a snowy scene on manila paper. Use a very watery blue wash over the picture for the crayon resist. Use a gray construction paper background for a cloudy scene. Add white cotton clouds, blue raindrops, and gold glitter for lightning.

Parent Letter

Dear Parents,

We are now working on a thematic unit about weather. We will do experiments and make observations as we learn about weather.

We will enjoy many factual and fictional books about weather including *What Will the Weather Be Like Today?* by Paul Rogers, *Rain* by Peter Spier, and *Cloudy with a Chance of Meatballs* by Judi Barrett.

Our variety of activities will cross the curriculum in science, reading, writing, math, social studies, art, and music. Please discuss with your child what we have done each day to reinforce our learning. Your child will bring home a little book of *Weather* to read with you. We have many interesting activities planned for this unit:

1. Observing and recording the weather and temperature each day on a Weather Observation Chart and Temperature Graph.
2. Recognizing the location of an area on the globe, and learning how the location of an area on the earth influences that area's weather.
3. Listing fun things to do on rainy days, snowy days, and hot days.
4. Making a Weather Headband.
5. Creating a Weather Wall filled with weather information.

We could use your help at home in two ways:

First, keep the chart below on your refrigerator and help your child observe the weather each morning and draw a symbol to tell what the predicted weather is for that day (sun, cloud, umbrella, snowflake, fog, or kite) on the chart; we'll use the same symbols on our Weather Observation Chart at school.

Second, help your child find articles about weather and pictures of weather maps in a newspaper, talk about them together, and then have your child bring them to school to include on our Weather Wall.

Thank you for your cooperation in helping your child learn about our world and its weather!

Sincerely,

Monday	Tuesday	Wednesday	Thursday	Friday

Weather

What kind of weather will we have today?

Must I stay indoors?

Can I go out to play?

It's hot today.

I'll play in the sun.

I'll wear my shorts and have lots of fun.

It's rainy today.

I won't get wet.

I'll take my umbrella and be all set.

It's snowing today.

My hat's on my head.

I'll wear mittens and boots when I ride on my sled.

It's windy today.

I have a cold nose.

I'm lucky I'm wearing my warmest clothes.

It's foggy today and so hard to see.

Be careful! Watch out!

Don't bump into me!

What kind of weather do we have today?

Must I stay indoors?

Can I go out to play?

Making Little Books

My Little Book of

Weather

Name_____

What kind of weather will we have today?

Must I stay indoors?

Can I go out to play?

1

Making Little Books *(cont.)*

It's hot today.

I'll play in the sun.

I'll wear my shorts and have lots of fun.

2

It's rainy today.

I won't get wet.

I'll take my umbrella and be all set.

3

Making Little Books *(cont.)*

It's snowing today.

My hat's on my head.

I'll wear mittens and boots

When I ride on my sled.

4

It's windy today.

I have a cold nose.

I'm lucky I'm wearing

My warmest clothes.

5

Making Little Books *(cont.)*

It's foggy today and so hard to see.

Be careful! Watch out!

Don't bump into me!

6

What kind of weather do we have today?

Must I stay indoors?

Can I go out to play?

7

Weather Observation Chart

Record the date. Use the symbols below to record the day's weather.

Date _____	Date _____
Date _____	Date _____
Date _____	Date _____
Date _____	Date _____
Date _____	Date _____

○ = Sunny   = Rainy   = Windy   = Cloudy   = Snowy   = Foggy

Weather Patterns

64

Weather Patterns *(cont.)*

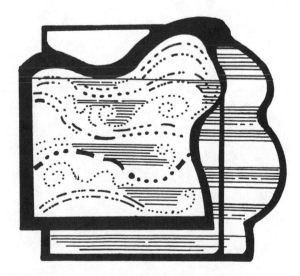

Pinwheel Pattern

Directions: Cut along the dashed lines. Bring all the corners marked "A" together to meet in the center. Pin the four bent-in corners through the center of the square dot. Push the pin into a pencil eraser. Blow on the pinwheel to test it.

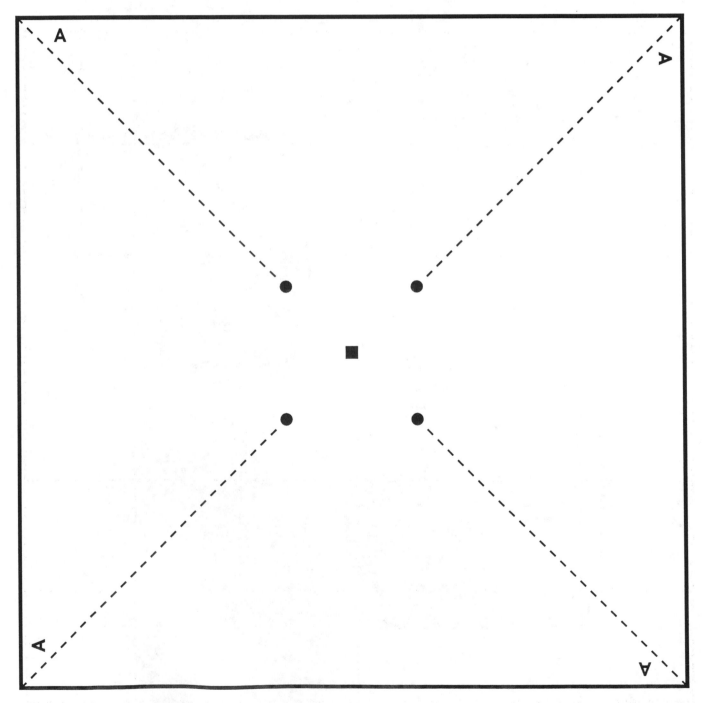

Patterns

What Will Our Weather Be Like Today?

Seasons

Featured Literature: *Caps, Hats, Socks, and Mittens:*
A Book About the Four Seasons

Author: Louise Borden

Publisher: Scholastic, 1989

Summary: This book uses simple text and illustrations to celebrate familiar activities which take place in each of the four seasons.

Additional Literature: *The Berenstain Bears Four Seasons* by Jan and Stan Berenstain (Random House, 1991); *The Seasons of Arnold's Apple Tree* by Gail Gibbons (HBJ, 1984); *Spring, Winter, Summer, Fall,* a series by Fionna Pragoff (Macmillan, 1993); *How Do You Know It's Fall?* a series by Allan Fowler (Children's Press, 1991, 1992); *Seasons* by David Bennett (Bantam, 1988); *Sunshine Makes the Seasons* by Franklyn M. Branley (Harper & Row, 1985); *Red Leaf, Yellow Leaf* by Lois Ehlert (HBJ, 1991).

Related Songs: "Four Seasons" by Mrs. Bill Dean, "Winter, Spring, Summer, Fall," by Judi Hall, and "Summer, Fall, Winter, Spring" by Saundra Winnett, *More Piggyback Songs* (Warren Publishing House, 1984).

Day 1: First, discuss the title and cover of the book. Ask students to name the four seasons. Explain that "fall" and "autumn" mean the same season. Look carefully at the illustrations on the cover and identify the season each depicts. Discuss why the author used "Caps, Hats, Socks, and Mittens" as part of the title for the book. Read the book; encourage children to share comments: "Oh, I've done that!" etc.

If your locale does not have distinct seasonal changes, include additional literature selections to build students' knowledge, such as the series of books by Fionna Pragoff and the series by Allan Fowler.

After reading *Caps, Hats, Socks, and Mittens*, have your class make a list of things the children did in each separate season. Read the book again, encouraging children to join in on your rereading.

Present the poem "Four Seasons" to your class using an overhead transparency or chart. Read the poem several times; have children fill in the second rhyming word in each two-line verse of the poem.

Reproduce page 82 so students can make a Mini-Book of Seasons to take home.

Send home the Parent Letter on page 72.

Seasons *(cont.)*

Day 1 *(cont.)*: Begin a group writing project with your students to create your own class book of seasons, *A Sampler of the Four Seasons*. Using the overhead or a sheet of chart paper, write the word "Winter" at the top. Write suggestions your students give about winter. Then ask the students to help you create a page of text about winter. You might want to begin with "Winter is..." and then add their suggestions, modeling your thinking processes on where to put capitals, periods, and where to begin new sentences. Say each word you write slowly, and exaggerate the sounds so children hear the letter sounds as you write them. Proceed with the other seasons in the same manner.

Reread the poem, "Four Seasons," using the flannel board shapes (pages 78-81). Guide individual children to take turns in adding the flannel board shapes at the appropriate times. Put your flannel board shapes and a copy of the poem at your Reading Center.

Let each child make a little book of the poem by reproducing pages 74-77 for each child. Assemble and use the books as explained on page 4.

Day 2: Begin today by reading *Caps, Hats, Socks, and Mittens*, encouraging your students to read along with you as often as possible. Reread the book several times, and discuss how it is organized into categories: winter, spring, summer, and fall.

Day 3: Introduce other literature about the four seasons to your students today. *The Seasons of Arnold's Apple Tree* is a delightful classic that describes the changes of an apple tree during the four seasons. The Lois Ehlert book *Red Leaf, Yellow Leaf* beautifully illustrates the variety of colorful fall leaves. After reading these books, point out that some trees (apple, maple, oak, etc.) are deciduous trees, which means they lose their leaves in the fall. However, evergreen trees do not lose their leaves (needles) in the fall and remain green all year round, hence their name.

Choose a real tree outside your school or classroom window, if possible, to observe throughout the entire school year. For fun, take a photograph of your students beside the tree during each of the four seasons to show the changes which occur.

Read *The Berenstain Bears Four Seasons* for another description of seasonal changes.

Reread the poem "Four Seasons" today using the overhead and flannel board shapes.

Try to finish your group writing project today. Begin by having your students think of ideas to tell about the last two seasons following directions given for Day 2.

Make a graph called "What Is Your Favorite Season?" Children can color, cut out, and glue on the seasonal shapes on pages 83 and 84 to label each of the columns on your graph.

Seasons *(cont.)*

Day 4: Begin today by rereading some of the literature already read, as well as the poem "Four Seasons." *Seasons* by David Bennett and *Sunshine Makes the Seasons* are good to use with young students.

To illustrate the revolution of the earth around the sun have one child hold a large classroom ball (yellow, if possible) to represent the sun, and explain that this child will not move, because the sun does not move. Hold the classroom globe and walk its orbit around the sun, tilting the globe appropriately and stopping to identify the position of the earth for each of the four seasons. (Note: If age-appropriate, explain that due to the tilting of the earth, some places on earth have winter while others have summer; some places on earth have fall while others have spring. Demonstrate this with the ball and globe.)

Copy the text of your class book onto 18" x 24" (46 cm x 61 cm) sheets of paper; leave space for illustrations. Reread your group writing project, *A Sampler of the Four Seasons*, several times. Have groups illustrate each page; have one group do a cover. Make the last page a "Give Yourself Credit" page, "Written and Illustrated by..." Have each child sign his or her name to show that everyone had an important part in the creation of the book.

Day 5: Reread the poem, "Four Seasons," and your students' favorite seasonal literature. Encourage students to listen for seasonal images they will need on their next project.

Divide your students into four groups to create a mural of the four seasons on a very long sheet of bulletin board paper divided into four sections. You can use four separate sheets of bulletin board paper, one for each season. Discuss again what might be included in each section. When completed, display the mural prominently at your science center.

To conclude your unit about seasons, have a "Seasonal Celebration" for another class or for the parents. Have children dressed for various seasons and recite appropriate sections of the poem, "Four Seasons."

Display your group writing project, *A Sampler of the Four Seasons*, on your classroom wall. Read your story for your guests.

Tell your guests about your mural with good oral language.

For snacks, try a "Seasonal Smorgasbord" such as hot chocolate (winter), ice cream and watermelon (summer), apple slices (fall), and strawberries (spring).

Sing some of the suggested seasonal songs for your guests. Teach the songs to your guests, using the overhead or chart, and have them join in a "Seasonal Sing-Along!"

Seasons Centers

Reading Center: Make available copies of *Caps, Hats, Socks, and Mittens* (also available as a big book), plus additional literature selections. Have class use the overhead projector and flannel board for independent or group reading of the poem, "Four Seasons." Display your wall story, *A Sampler of the Four Seasons*, on the wall here; later your wall story may be made it into a class book. Display completed take-home assignments prominently at this center. Read and admire each, as it is brought back to school.

Writing Center: Children can make their own pages to add to a set of class books about the four seasons. Use pages 83-84 to create covers for four class books: Wonderful Winter, Sparkling Spring, Sizzling Summer, and Fabulous Fall. Have children write a sentence on each page beginning with "I am..." (telling what they like to do in that season) and then draw themselves doing it. At the end of your unit, bind the children's pages with the covers into the class books.

Math Center: Set up estimating jars for this unit — one for each of the four seasons: for Winter, use cotton balls to represent snowballs; for Spring, use candy or plastic eggs; for Summer, use plastic bicycles (available from Oriental Trading, see page 56 for address); for Fall, use crayons to represent going to school.

Have a clothes basket of different types of seasonal clothing for children to sort according to the appropriate wearing season. (Your school's "Lost and Found" may be a good source of clothing items.) Use two hoops on the floor, resembling a Venn diagram, in which children sort. Make season labels for the sorting. Do some sample sorting with your students to prepare them for working independently. Encourage students to note which clothing articles can be worn more than one season.

Science Center: Keep your classroom ball, which was the sun in your demonstration, and the classroom globe at this center to allow children to demonstrate why the seasons occur. Explain that the earth's revolution around the sun takes one entire year, 365 days, so it is important to move slowly around the sun.

Display your mural of the four seasons.

Have available a variety of good informational books about the seasons. Your school library or public library will have several in addition to the ones suggested previously in this unit.

Encourage children to use creativity and variety to portray different seasons around the home. They can pretend to pick vegetables from the garden and clean them for dinner; they can wear summer clothing, turn on a pretend fan or air conditioner, or play in the sprinkler. If you have a sand table, bring in beach toys for the children to use. (If you don't have a sand table, bring in a small wading pool for sand or for water activities.)

Art Center: Encourage children to create paintings of the beautiful qualities of each season; display paintings, grouped according to season.

Parent Letter

Dear Parents,

We are currently working on a thematic unit called "Our Four Seasons." We will learn the names of the seasons, how the earth goes around the sun to make our seasons, and the wonderful experiences we can have in each season.

We will read several good fictional and informational books about the four seasons, such as *Caps, Hats, Socks, and Mittens: A Book About the Four Seasons* by Louise Borden and *The Seasons of Arnold's Apple Tree* by Gail Gibbons.

Our seasonal activities will extend into science, reading, math, writing, art, and music. Discuss with your child what we learned each day and reinforce our learning. Your child will bring home a little book of a poem, "Four Seasons," to read with you. We will have interesting activities about seasons:

1. Demonstrating how the earth goes around the sun to make the four seasons.

2. Completing a group writing project to create a class wall story called *A Sampler of the Four Seasons*.

3. Making a graph of our favorite seasons.

4. Observing a tree on the school grounds throughout the changing seasons.

5. Creating a mural of the four seasons.

Discuss the four seasons at home with your child. Then choose one favorite family activity you enjoy during one particular season. Complete the sentence at the bottom of this page with your child, and have your child illustrate the sentence. Have your child bring this back to school to display at our reading center.

Thank you for your help with this project!

Sincerely,

In the _____ , I like to _____ .

Name _____

Four Seasons

Earth changes seasons, four in all:

Winter, spring, summer, fall.

Winter is cold when North Winds blow.

I stay inside and watch it snow.

Spring's dark clouds bring lots of showers.

Giving drinks to growing flowers.

Summer's sun burns bright and strong.

Vacation days are hot and long.

Trees drop leaves when fall turns cool.

And that's when we go back to school.

Winter, spring, summer, fall.

Earth has four seasons; I like them all!

Making Little Books

My Little Book of
Four Seasons

Name _____

Earth changes seasons, four in all:

Winter, spring, summer, fall.

1

Making Little Books *(cont.)*

Winter is cold when North Winds blow.

I stay inside and watch it snow.

2

Spring's dark clouds bring lots of showers.

Giving drinks to growing flowers.

3

Making Little Books *(cont.)*

Summer's sun burns bright and strong.

Vacation days are hot and long.

4

Trees drop leaves when fall turns cool.

And that's when we go back to school.

5

Making Little Books *(cont.)*

Winter, spring, summer, fall.

Earth has four seasons; I like them all!

6

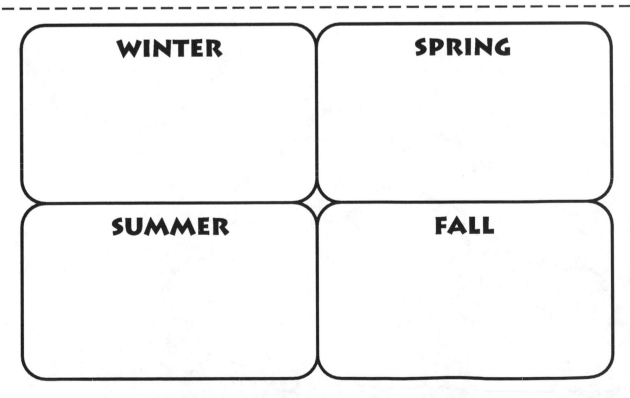

WINTER	SPRING
SUMMER	FALL

I like winter, spring, summer, and fall.

7

Patterns

78

Patterns *(cont.)*

SCHOOL

Patterns *(cont.)*

Patterns *(cont.)*

Winter

Spring

Summer

Fall

Mini-Book of Seasons

MY MINI-BOOK OF
SEASONS

By _____

1

It is winter.

2

It snows in the winter.

3

It is spring.

4

It rains in the spring.

5

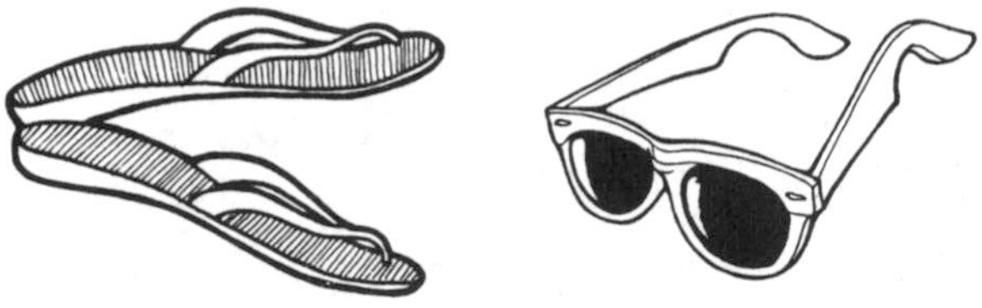

It is summer.

6

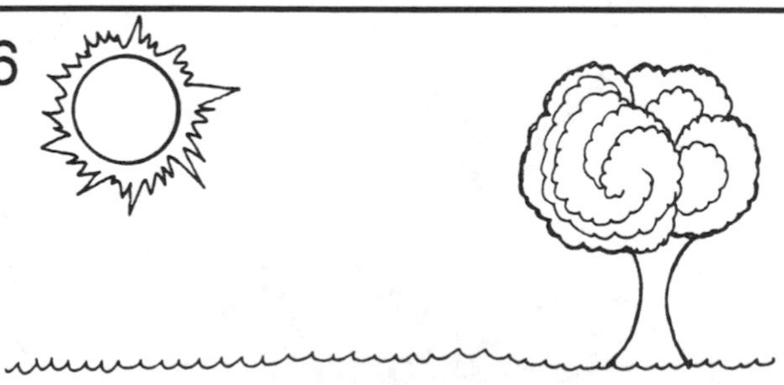

It is hot in the summer.

7

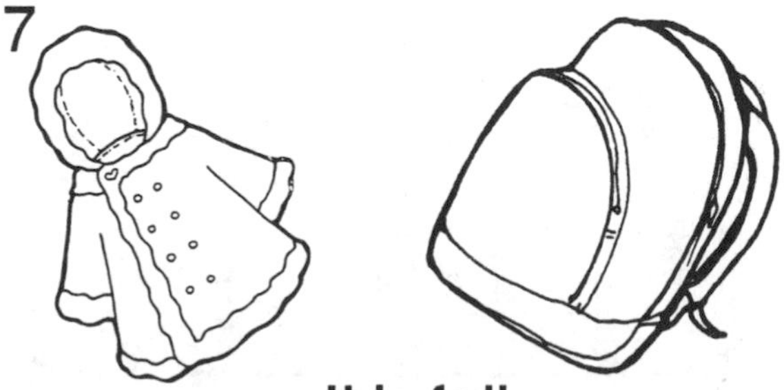

It is fall.

8

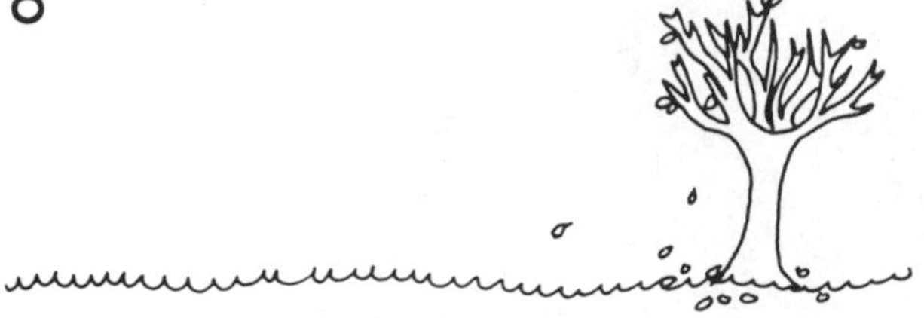

Leaves fall in the fall.

9

There are four seasons —
winter, spring, summer, and fall.

Seasonal Patterns

Seasonal Patterns (cont.)

84

Seeds and Plants

Featured Literature: *The Tiny Seed*

Author: Eric Carle

Publisher: Picture Book Studio, 1987

Summary: This beautifully illustrated book follows one tiny seed, blown by the wind in autumn, through winter and into spring when it takes root and grows into a gigantic flower in summer. As the story ends, it is autumn again, and the flower is a source of new seeds blown by the wind.

Additional Literature: *How a Seed Grows* by Helene J. Jordan (HarperCollins, 1992); *A Seed Is a Promise* by Claire Merrill (Scholastic, 1973); *From Seed to Plant* by Gail Gibbons (Holiday House, 1991); *One Watermelon Seed* by Celia Baker Lottridge (Oxford University Press, 1985); *The Enormous Watermelon* retold by Brenda Parkes and Judith Smith (Rigby, 1988); *The Reason for a Flower* by Ruth Heller (Putnam, 1983); *Rabbit Seeds* by Bijou Le Tord (Dell, 1984).

Related Songs: "I'll Plant a Little Seed" by Leora Grecian and "Flower Garden" by Nancy H. Giles, *Piggyback Songs* (Warren Publishing House, 1983); "The Garden Song" by Kathleen M. Todd and "The Seed" by Adele Engelbracht, *More Piggyback Songs* (Warren Publishing House, 1984)

Day 1: First, learn what your students already know about seeds and plants. You'll need three large seed shapes cut from construction paper to make a K-W-L display. Write "What We Already Know" on the first, and list information about seed and plants your students already know (K). Write "What We Want to Find Out" on the second, and record what (W) your students want to find out. Write "What We Learned" on the third, and leave to complete on the last day of the unit. Display the lists in your science center.

Read *The Tiny Seed* to your class, calling attention to the seasons mentioned and to the circle aspect of the story — indicating the repetitive life cycle.

Present the "Seeds Chant" to your class using an overhead transparency or chart. Have students follow along as you read. Use the flannel board shapes (pages 95-97) to give students clues as to which plant comes next in the chant. Reread the chant again, encouraging your students to join in. Give individual children the flannel board shapes and have them place the shapes on the flannel board to match the words of the chant as you read along.

Read aloud *How a Seed Grows*. Have students listen to learn what seeds and plants need in order to grow (soil, water, and sun).

Send home the Parent Letter on page 89.

Seeds and Plants *(cont.)*

Day 2: Re-read *The Tiny Seed* and the "Seeds Chant." Have children use their prediction and memory skills and the flannel board shapes to join in while you read. Make sentence strips of the chant and use in a pocket chart; add to your reading center.

Follow the directions found in *How A Seed Grows* for planting twelve bean seeds in an egg carton. Record the class observations of the seed growth on a large sheet of chart paper; include the date, a short sentence describing the experiment, and a simple sketch.

Have your students brainstorm a list of food items that grow in a garden. Make a graph of favorite foods that grow in a garden. Display both in your science center.

Introduce the Mother Goose rhyme "Mary, Mary, Quite Contrary" to your students. After they seem confident with the pattern and rhyme, create innovations using the names of your students and real garden items. Hold up 3" x 5" (8 cm x 13 cm) index cards with your students' names such as "Jenna, Jenna quite contrary" as you do your innovations, so children will learn to recognize their own names and the names of their classmates.

Day 3: Read *The Enormous Watermelon*. Ask students to predict which Mother Goose characters will appear next in the story using the picture clues. *One Watermelon Seed* leads children into counting, and introduces a variety of garden items. *Rabbit Seeds* is a fun story for young children. *The Reason for a Flower*, *From Seed to Plant*, and *A Seed Is a Promise*, all provide more information for your young scientists.

Read the "Seeds Chant" with your students. Let each child make a little book of the chant by reproducing pages 91-94 for each child. Assemble and use the books as explained on page 4.

Discuss the basic needs which all plants have (soil, water, and sun). Give each child a disposable clear-plastic cup. Have children print their names on pieces of masking tape to label their cups. Fill the cup ⅔ full with potting soil. Have each child count out 20 wheat kernels; then sprinkle with enough additional soil to only cover them. (If the seeds are planted too deeply, it will take too long to show growth.) Help each child water the seeds lightly, then place cups in your Science Center near the egg carton experiment. Wheat sprouts very rapidly, and you'll be able to see the roots growing through the clear cup within a day or two. Green growth will appear very soon thereafter. The teacher may wish to prepare a set of seeds to test various growing conditions: plant two sets as above and put one in a closet so it gets no sunlight and one in a sunny location, but do not water. Put another set of seeds in a cup with water only and place in a sunny location. Observe what happens to these seeds over time; compare the progress of the children's seeds.

Use a large sheet of chart paper to record your wheat planting and growing. Include the date, a short sentence, a simple sketch. Children may record this in a science journal. See page 144.

Seeds and Plants *(cont.)*

Day 4: Read the "Seeds Chant" using flannel board shapes. Reread *The Enormous Watermelon*, with students joining in whenever possible.

Dig up one bean seed to see if it has sprouted. (You can dig up a different bean seed every two to three days, because they will grow above the soil before you've dug up too many.) Check the progress of your wheat seeds. Record observations on charts, and have children update science journals.

Ask the children what three things all plants need. Have the children dictate a sentence for you to write on chart paper (e.g., "All plants neeed soil, water, and sun."). Put this sentence at your Reading Center. Make word cards of the individual words from this sentence on index cards so children can practice building the sentence.

Give each child a copy of page 98 and a strip of paper that is 8" x 24" (20 x 60 cm). Children are to color the four stages of the life of a plant, cut out the four boxes, and then glue them onto the strip from left to right in correct sequence. At the top of the page, have children copy the sentence you wrote together.

Extend literature selections into classroom centers. See page 88.

Day 5: On the third seed shape, record what your students learned during this unit on seeds and plants.

Have a Garden Party to culminate your unit on seeds and plants. Discuss the different kinds of gardens: flower, vegetable, fruit. Visit a nearby garden or garden center to learn more about seeds and plants. If possible, plant a vegetable garden on school grounds. (This is a great all-school project and a terrific way to learn!) Or try planting a variety of vegetable seeds in different containers inside your classroom; create labels for your garden.

Have your students do a "Yes / No" graph for the question, "Do you have a garden at home?"

Reread *The Tiny Seed*; draw attention to the illustrations. Then have children add their own brightly colored flowers to a classroom garden mural.

As a healthy concluding snack, enjoy some fruits, such as apples, oranges, bananas, and grapes, since all these fruits grow from seeds. Divide the fruits into halves, thirds, and fourths, for a hands-on demonstration of fractions.

(Note: Keep your plants growing; continue observing and recording their growth progress, as long as children remain interested.)

Seeds and Plants Centers

Reading Center: Make available copies of the literature selections: use the overhead transparency of the "Seeds Chant;" use sentence strips in pocket chart; and use word cards of the plant to match sentence strips.

Writing Center: Have a variety of seed catalogs, seed packets, and plant books available for reference. Encourage students to design their own seed packets. Compile the seed packets into a class book, or display in your science center.

Math Center: Read *One Watermelon Seed* to your students to introduce them to a variety of seeds and counting. Have a variety of real seeds (apple, tomato, watermelon, acorns, etc.) available for sorting and counting. Use to make sequenced patterns and solve simple addition and subtraction problems.

Have a watermelon as a snack with your class and save the seeds. Let the seeds dry, and use in your estimating jar. Refer to *Connecting Science and Literature* (Teacher Created Materials #341) for class exercise in "Watermelon Math."

Science Center: Have children reread the K - W - L information found on the seed shapes at your science center. Children will enjoy observing the growth of the bean seeds. The wheat will grow rapidly and provide an opportunity for children to use a ruler to measure daily growth. Record observations on a class chart or in individual journals.

Start a variety of other plantings for children to observe: plant a pineapple top in soil; grow carrot tops in gravel; insert toothpicks into a avocado pit and submerse the bottom of the pit in water; put the bottom half of a sweet potato into a clear jar of water.

Begin a "Seed Chart" with real seeds the children bring from home; include names of the seeds and pictures of the vegetable or fruit.

Put up a poster showing the different parts of a plant. Reproduce page 99 for children to label the parts of a plant independently.

Dramatic Play Center: Provide a variety of gardening props. If you have a sand table, use props to demonstrate how to prepare soil before planting.

Art Center: Have children draw a shape, put glue in the shape, and then use seeds to fill in the shape to make seed pictures.

Use a variety of fruits and vegetables, such as carrots, potatoes, and apples, to make prints. Put several colors of tempera paints in disposable metal pie tins. Children dip the fruits and vegetables into the plant and make prints on sheets of paper. Model this procedure for your students first. Children can add words to tell what made the prints.

Parent Letter

Dear Parents,

We are currently working on a "Seeds and Plants" thematic unit. We will conduct several experiments with seeds to learn that all seeds and plants need soil, water, and sunlight to grow.

We will also enjoy several good books about seeds and plants: *The Tiny Seed* by Eric Carle, *How a Seed Grows* by Helene J. Jordan, and *The Reason for a Flower* by Ruth Heller.

Our activities about seeds and plants will cross many curriculum areas, including science, reading, math, writing, art, and music. Discuss with your child what was learned each day to reinforce the learning. Your child will bring home a little book of our "Seeds Chant" to read with you. We've planned interesting activities for this unit:

1. Planting bean seeds and checking on their progress each day.

2. Making a list of foods that grow in a garden.

3. Giving our wheat seeds soil, water, and sunlight, and observing what happens to the teacher's seeds that don't get soil, water, or sunlight.

4. Making a sequence strip of the stages of a plant.

5. Collecting real seeds and using them to create a "Seed Chart" at our Science Center.

During the next few days, please save any seeds you find in foods you prepare at your house, wash them, and send them to school in a disposable, plastic bag. It would help if you could attach a label telling us what kind of seeds you're sending. The children will use these seeds in math and art projects, for planting at our science center, and for adding to our Seed Chart. If you would like to send a packet of seeds, we could use those, too.

As an enrichment experience, you might take your child on a family field trip to a farmer's market or the produce section of your grocery store to look at the fresh fruits and vegetables. Discuss with your child whether these items grow on a tree, on a vine above the ground, or under the ground. A family field trip to a garden center to look at their variety of plants and seeds would also be a good learning experience.

Thank you for your cooperation in helping your child learn about seeds and plants!

Sincerely,

Seeds Chant

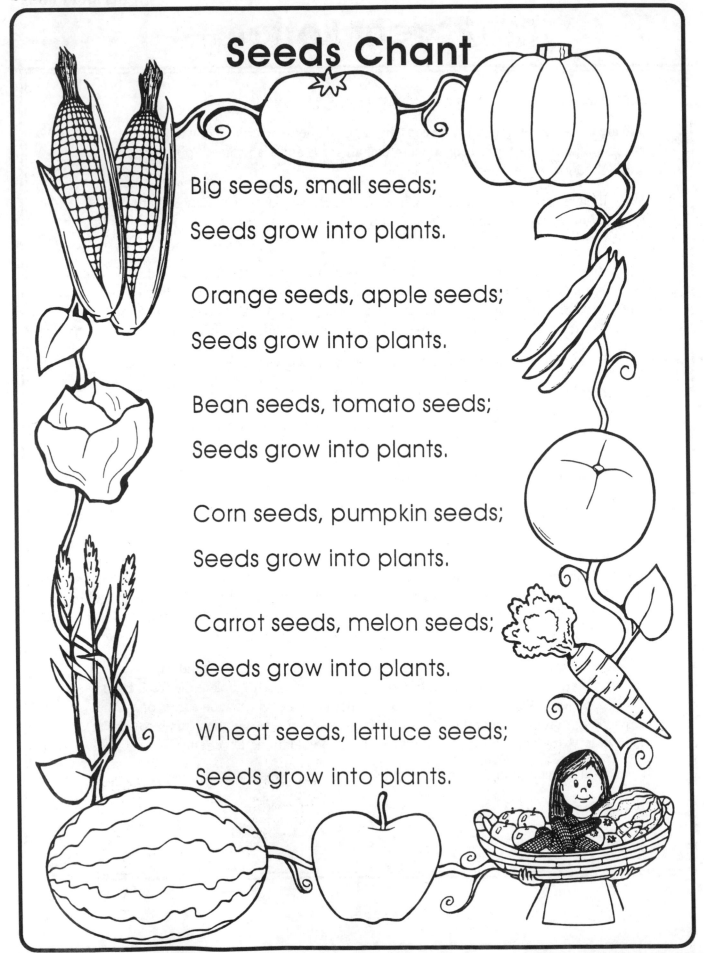

Big seeds, small seeds;

Seeds grow into plants.

Orange seeds, apple seeds;

Seeds grow into plants.

Bean seeds, tomato seeds;

Seeds grow into plants.

Corn seeds, pumpkin seeds;

Seeds grow into plants.

Carrot seeds, melon seeds;

Seeds grow into plants.

Wheat seeds, lettuce seeds;

Seeds grow into plants.

Making Little Books

- -

My Little Book of the

Seeds Chant

Name_____

- -

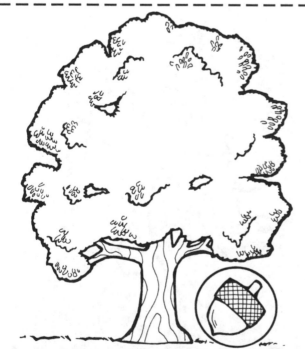

Big seeds, small seeds;

Seeds grow into plants.

1

- -

Making Little Books *(cont.)*

Orange seeds, apple seeds;

Seeds grow into plants.

2

Bean seeds, tomato seeds;

Seeds grow into plants.

3

Making Little Books *(cont.)*

Corn seeds, pumpkin seeds;

Seeds grow into plants.

4

Carrot seeds, melon seeds;

Seeds grow into plants.

5

Making Little Books *(cont.)*

 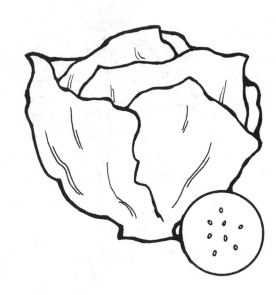

Wheat seeds, lettuce seeds;

Seeds grow into plants.

6

**Draw a picture of a seed
growing into a plant.**

7

Shapes

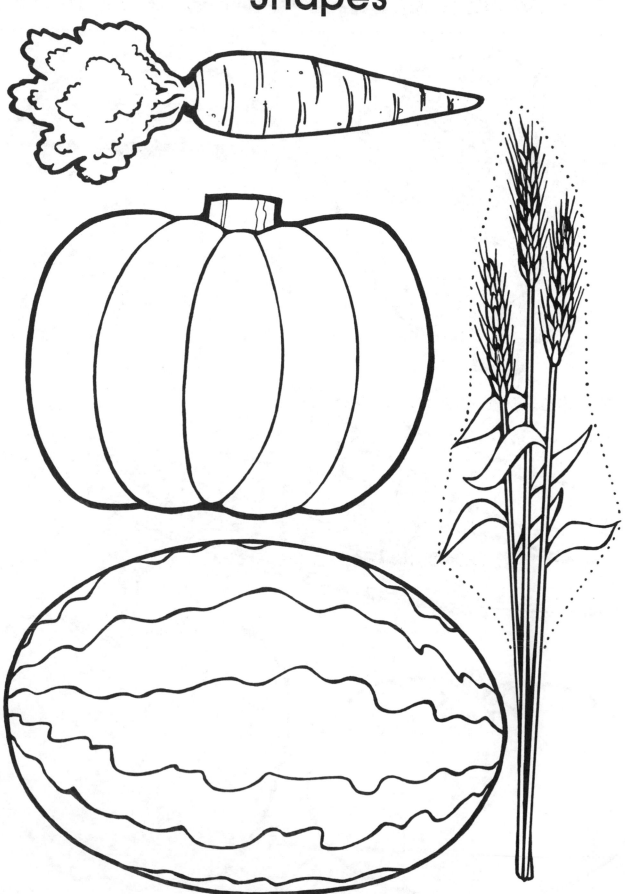

Shapes *(cont.)*

96

Shapes (cont.)

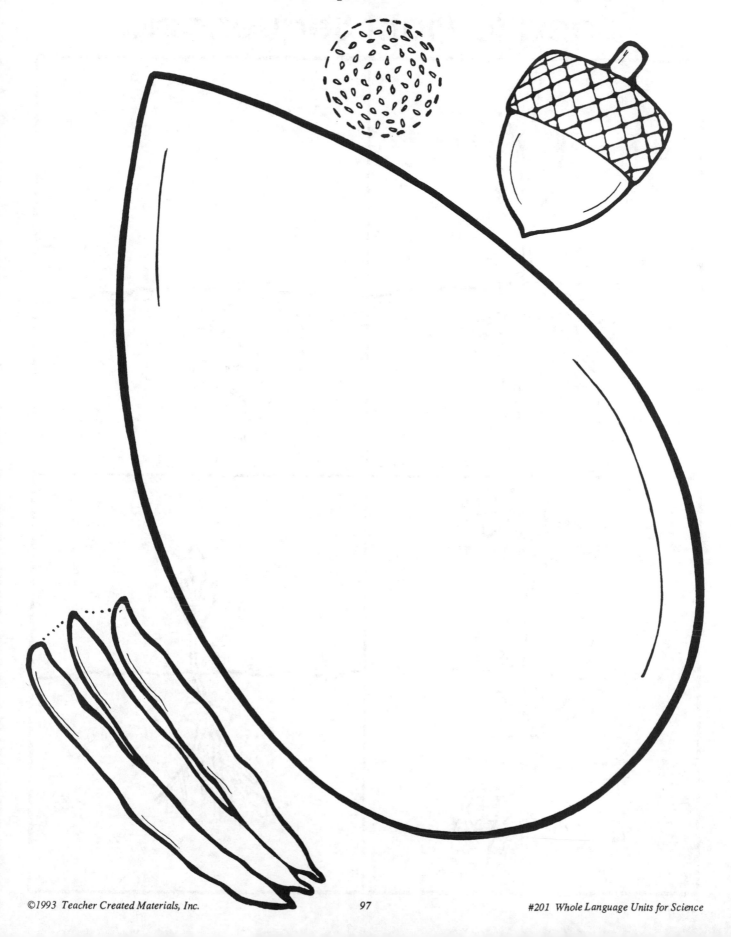

Name _____

Seed to Plant Sequencing

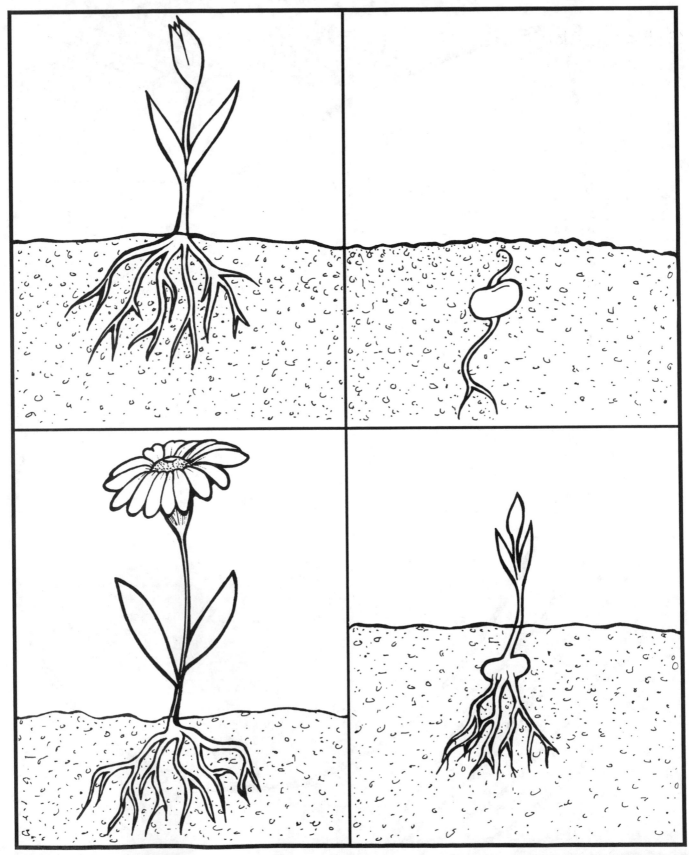

Name_____

Parts of a Plant

Color the plant. Cut along the dotted lines. Cut out the word labels. Match the words to the corresponding plant parts. Glue the labels in the word boxes.

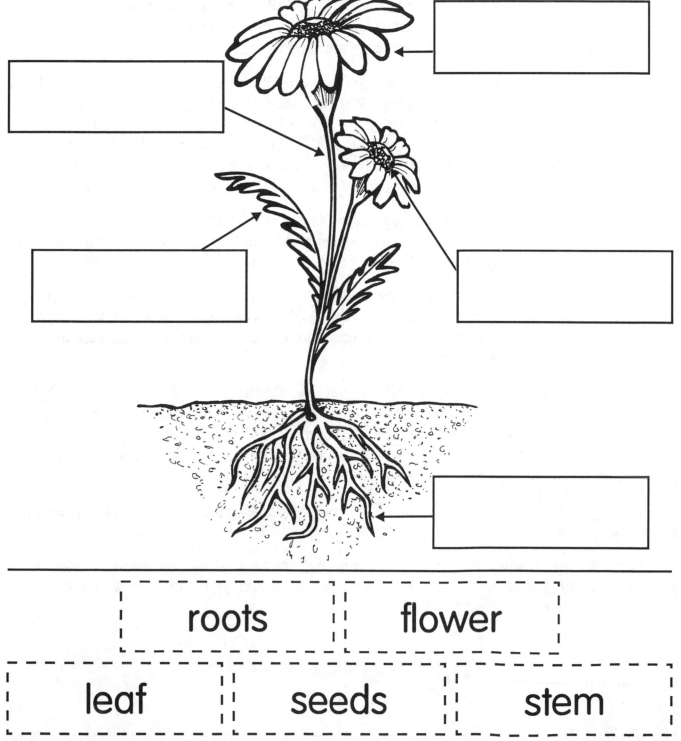

roots   flower

leaf   seeds   stem

Eggs

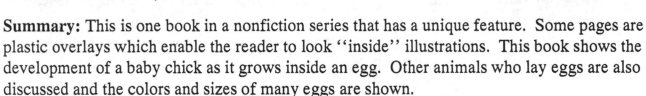

Featured Literature: *The Egg*

Author: Gallimard Jeunesse and Pascale de Bourgoing

Publisher: Scholastic, Inc. 1989

Summary: This is one book in a nonfiction series that has a unique feature. Some pages are plastic overlays which enable the reader to look "inside" illustrations. This book shows the development of a baby chick as it grows inside an egg. Other animals who lay eggs are also discussed and the colors and sizes of many eggs are shown.

Additional Literature: *Chickens Aren't the Only Ones* by Ruth Heller (Scholastic, Inc. 1981); *The Chicken Book* by Garth Williams (Dell, 1970); *Hatched from An Egg* by Joanne Nelson (Modern Curriculum Press, 1990); *Good Morning, Chick* by Mirra Ginsburg (Mulberry Books, 1980); *Whose Eggs Are These?* by Brian and Jillian Cutting (Wright Group, 1988); *Green Eggs and Ham* by Dr. Seuss (Random House, 1960); *Animals Born Alive and Well* by Ruth Heller (Scholastic, 1987); *See How They Grow: Chicks* by Jane Burton (Dorling Kindersley, 1991).

Related Songs: "I'm a Little Chicken" by Susan Peters, *Holiday Piggyback Songs* (Warren Publishing House, 1988); "Look At All The Chickens" by Cindy Dingwell and "The Chicken Family" by Carla C. Skjong, *Animal Piggyback Songs* (Warren Publishing House, 1990).

Day 1: Before reading the featured selection to the class, cut a large egg shape out of tagboard. Write "What Hatches From Eggs?" on it. Ask the children what animals they think hatch from eggs. Write all answers on the egg shape with one color of marker; put a question mark next to any of the children who are unsure.

Read the story, drawing attention to the plastic overlays. Define the word "oviparous," which means "hatches from eggs." Go back to the large egg shape and put a star next to the animals mentioned in the book. Use a different color marker to add any new animals named in the book, but not on the original list. Cross out any animals that do not hatch from eggs (or do this at a later time after researching answers). Save the list for future use.

Read the "Eggs" poem on page 106. Enlarge the poem on chart paper or prepare sentence strips for the pocket chart.

Send home the parent letter explaining the surprise egg activity. Attach a small plastic egg in a self-sealing plastic bag to each letter. Prepare a large plastic egg as a surprise egg for the classroom (see the center description on page 102).

Eggs *(cont.)*

Consider having a real hatching experiment! Obtain some chicken eggs, which hatch in about 21 days, from a farm supplier or university agriculture program. Gather supplies: incubator (preferably with an automatic turner), food, a water bottle, and a brooder for the newborn chicks. Incubators in a range of sizes and prices are available from Nasco, P.O. Box 901, Fort Atkinson, WI 53538-0901. Tel: 1 (800) 558-9595.

Day 2: Today, learn about the parts of an egg: shell, membrane, albumen, yolk, and germ spot. Use the diagram found on page 114 to teach the children these new words. Working in small groups, crack open some real eggs into plastic bowls and find all the parts. Try some simple egg experiments, such as spinning an egg to find out if it is raw or hard-boiled. You might also trying floating an egg in plain water and then in salt water (salt water makes the egg buoyant so it floats).

Recite the classic Mother Goose rhyme, ''Humpty Dumpty.'' This rhyme provides a great opportunity to talk about cause and effect. Read *Who's Hatching Today?* or *Chickens Aren't the Only Ones* and see if you can add to your brainstorming list. Have the children draw or paint their favorite opivarous animal. These can be displayed with a sentence written underneath, such as ''A snake hatches from an egg.''

Introduce two ''eggy'' games today. Play ''Chicken, chicken where's your egg?'' like the classic game ''Doggie, doggie where's your bone? The children sit in a circle; one child in the center is "It." While that child's eyes are closed, a plastic egg is hidden in the hands of one of the children. The children chant ''Chicken, chicken where's your egg?'' and the child who is It gets three guesses to find the egg.

Another daily game for this unit is ''Who's Hatching Today?'' Display a large egg shape and each day hide a picture of a different oviparous animal underneath. Give the children three clues about the animal and have them guess the animal of the day. The clues can be given orally, or written next to the egg. Encourage children to write their guesses on the egg (laminate the egg shape and use a wipe-off marker).

Day 3: Read the "Eggs" poem again and have the children make the little book (see pages 107 to 110).

Gather the class together for a shared reading of *The Chicken Book* which has a good pattern and talks about ordinal numbers (the first chick, second chick etc.). Act out the story with chick stick puppets (shapes on page 115); the children may want to make a set of chicks to take home so they can retell the story.

Eggs *(cont.)*

Talk about the different ways that eggs are prepared as food. Make a picture graph of the children's favorite ways of eating eggs. Head each column with a picture of different kinds of eggs: scrambled, fried, hard-boiled. Children can indicate choices by signing their name on an egg shape and placing it in the appropriate column.

Day 4: If you are hatching chicken eggs, have the children observe and record or draw what they see and learn during this unit. When the eggs hatch, have the children vote on names for the chicks. Send home the birth announcement on page 111. Also send a birth announcement to your principal so your exciting news is included in the daily announcements. Have a chick open house and invite family members to come in to see your brood. Take excerpts from the children's chick journals to put together a newsletter of the experience to send home to parents.

Take photographs of various stages during the chick life-cycle experience. Use these photographs as the illustrations for a class book. Mount the photographs in a blank book and have the children dictate sentences to describe each photo. Be sure to include photos of the children playing with the chicks. Reproduce pages 112 and 113 for children to make booklets of the life cycles of a chick.

Introduce the learning centers for this theme. Read *Rechenka's Eggs*; and, if possible, bring in some beautiful pysanky, Ukranian Easter eggs. You might find someone to come to your classroom to demonstrate the art of decorating eggs. If not, try having the class dye and decorate some eggs with crayon patterns.

Day 5: Finish this "eggs-citing" theme with one of these ideas: Have a "Green-Eggs-and-Ham Breakfast" and invite parents. Prepare this unusual breakfast after reading the book by Dr. Seuss. Have the children design their own invitations for this event.

When the surprise eggs are brought in, read each child's clues and let the class guess what is in each egg. They may record their guesses in invented spelling or draw their guesses. Each child should have a turn to make a guess about what's in the class surprise egg (prepared by the teacher and placed at the math center). Reveal the items in that egg and count them, grouping by tens and ones.

Have your class perform *The Little Red Hen* as a culminating activity. If you have hatched chicks, include them as performers at the end of the play (students can hold several of them in their hands as the mother hen calls her chicks).

      102

Egg Centers

Reading Center: Have a display of both fiction and nonfiction books about hens, eggs, and chicks. Include some books about other types of birds so children can start to compare birds by their many different characteristics: color, feeding and nesting habits, size, and differences in eggs. Put out hen and chick puppets which are available commercially at many children's stores or make some simple stick puppets. Have available copies of *The Little Red Hen* or *The Chicken Book* and invite children to enact the stories. Both stories could also be told on a flannel board.

Make some extra copies of the "Eggs" poem and small book for use in this center.

Writing Center: Have children create their own ''What's Hatching From The Egg?'' riddles. This activity was introduced to the whole group during the unit. Have the names of the animals on the big egg shape posted in the center so children can choose an animal to write about. Invite the children to write stories about the animals, or they may want to try writing a nonfiction book which gives facts about one of the oviparous animals. Teacher should model the writing activities as a group story before this center is introduced.

Encourage the children to keep daily track of the hatching experience in a chick journal. Have a date stamp available so they can date their work, write a few words or sentences about what happened with the chicks, and illustrate. For a journal format, see pages 144.

Prepare a cover for a class book. Each child can contribute a page telling something he or she learned about chicks or eggs. Some possible titles for the books might be ''Chicksville U.S.A.'' or ''Chick Corners.''

Math Center: Make an egg number matching game by cutting egg shapes out of tagboard; number them 0-10; and laminate them. (Game may be adapted to focus on math facts, specific numbers, number words, or whatever you want the children to work on.) Sequence eggs, then have the children count out an appropriate number of corn kernels to place on each egg for the chick to eat when it is hatched (dried corn can be purchased at a feed or pet store).

In your estimating jar, place tiny plastic eggs or chocolate eggs. Have children write estimates on a large laminated egg shape. Count the eggs to check your estimates, grouping by tens and ones.

Egg Centers *(cont.)*

Math Center *(cont.)*: A surprise egg can also be at the math center for estimating work. The teacher fills a large plastic egg with a variety of small objects. Place the egg in a basket with some Easter grass or shredded tissue paper. The children not only estimate how many objects might be in the egg, but they also need to guess what items could be in the egg, considering its size.

For practice in measuring quantities, fill a large tub with dried corn. Provide a variety of containers, spoons, and measuring cups so children can experiment with volume. Also put out some balance scales and some plastic eggs so children can compare weights. Fill some of the eggs with corn and weigh them; balance a number of plastic eggs on one side of the scale with a quantity of corn on the other side of the scale.

Science Centers: If you are conducting a real hatching experience, set up supplies in your science area. Allow children to visit this area during the 21 days to look at the incubator, help with candling the eggs (using a candler with a light to look inside the developing eggs), and write observations in their journals. Have available books about hatching chicks, as well as some bird feathers, nests, and magnifying glasses for looking at them.

Dramatic Play Center: Set up a small picket fence around your play area (available at garden stores) to create a farm atmosphere. Add a play barn with small plastic farm animals or some stuffed animals. Put out some farm overalls and hats for the children to wear. Be sure to include some play eggs in cartons for cooking those hearty farm breakfasts. Place stuffed animal chickens in nests so children can pretend to gather eggs and feed the chickens.

Art Center: If you are hatching chicks, have the children create a barnyard scene to decorate your chick area. Use a sheet of blue construction paper for the background and add green and brown for the grass and ground. Children can do some sponge painting on white paper with yellow paint; when the paint is dry, cut out a chick shape. Use construction paper to add eyes, beak, and feet. Glue on some yellow feathers to add realistic effect (available at craft stores). Glue the chicks on the background paper and add a barn and other details to create a farm scene. Add speech bubbles over the chicks which say, "I predict I will hatch on _____" and add the date each child predicts.

After the chicks hatch, the children may want to make posters and signs welcoming the chicks and listing the chick's names, such as "Welcome, Fluffy."

Parent Letter

Dear Parents,

Our class will soon be involved in a special science unit on eggs. During this unit we will participate in many activities, such as learning the parts of an egg, reenacting the story of *The Little Red Hen*, and learning about animals which hatch from eggs. Your child is bringing home an activity which requires your participation. Your child received one empty ''surprise'' egg and needs to do the following with you:

1. Find a single object to put in the egg.

2. Have your child tell you three clues about the object. Write the sentences on the clue sheet.

3. Place the clue sheet and the egg in the plastic bag and return it to school by _____.

When the eggs are returned to school, we will read the riddles together and guess what is in each egg. The children draw or write their guesses (in their own spelling). We will also have a large surprise egg in our math center. The children will estimate how many objects could fit in that egg, as well as predict what items are in the egg.

Thanks for your help with our ''surprise eggs.''

Sincerely,

Please return this sheet with your egg by _____

What's in My Surprise Egg?

Clue 1 _____

_____

Clue 2 _____

_____

Clue 3 _____

_____

Egg Expert _____

Eggs

Eggs come in many sizes.

Eggs hold some big surprises.

Speckled, brown, white, or blue,

Eggs hold babies that are new.

Chicks from eggs are fluffy yellow.

Chicks from eggs are funny fellows!

106

Making Little Books

- -

My Little Book of

Eggs

Name_____

- -

Eggs come in many sizes.

1

- -

Making Little Books *(cont.)*

- -

Eggs hold some big surprises.

2

- -

Speckled, brown, white, or blue,

3

- -

Making Little Books *(cont.)*

- -

Eggs hold babies that are new.   **4**

- -

Chicks from eggs are fluffy yellow.   **5**

- -

Making Little Books *(cont.)*

Chicks from eggs are funny fellows!

6

Count the chicks and color them yellow.

7

the arrival of our baby chicks!

Date of Birth: _____

Place of Birth: _____

Room: _____

Number of Chicks: _____

Chicks' Names: _____

_____

A Picture of Our Chicks

Mini-Book

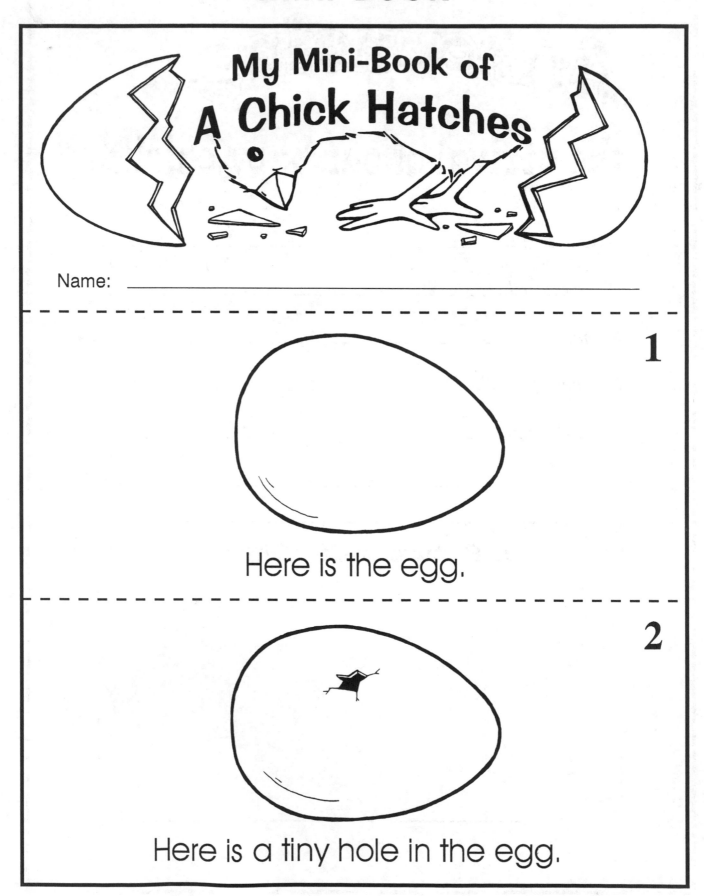

My Mini-Book of
A Chick Hatches

Name: _____

1

Here is the egg.

2

Here is a tiny hole in the egg.

Mini-Book *(cont.)*

3

Here is a bigger hole in the egg.

4

Here is the baby chick. It is wet.

5

Here is the baby chick.
Now it is dry and fluffy.

The Inside of an Egg

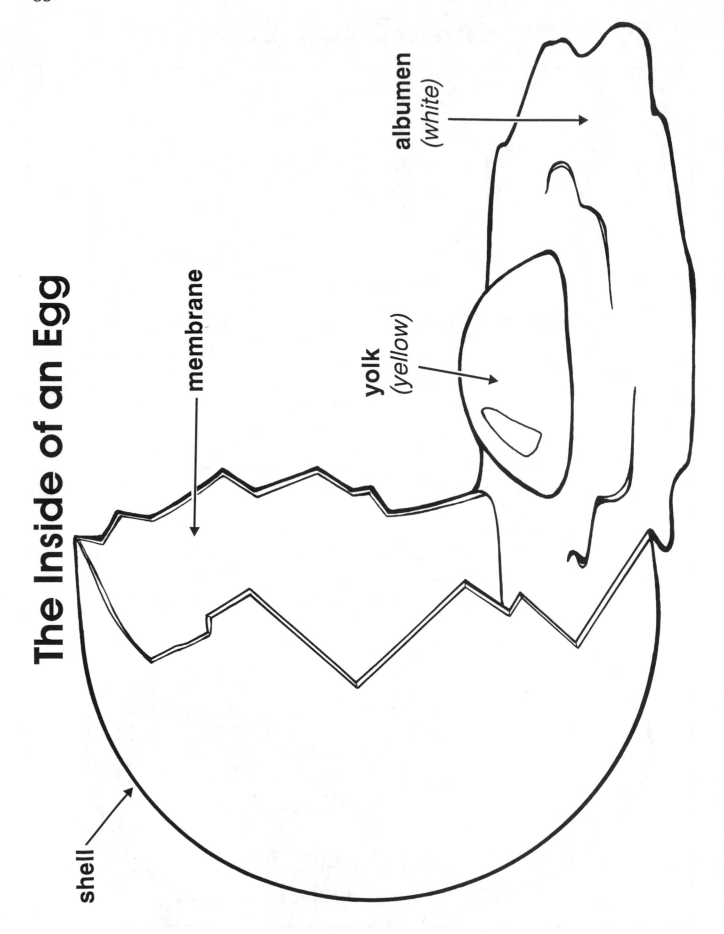

albumen
(white)

membrane

yolk
(yellow)

shell

Egg and Chick Shapes

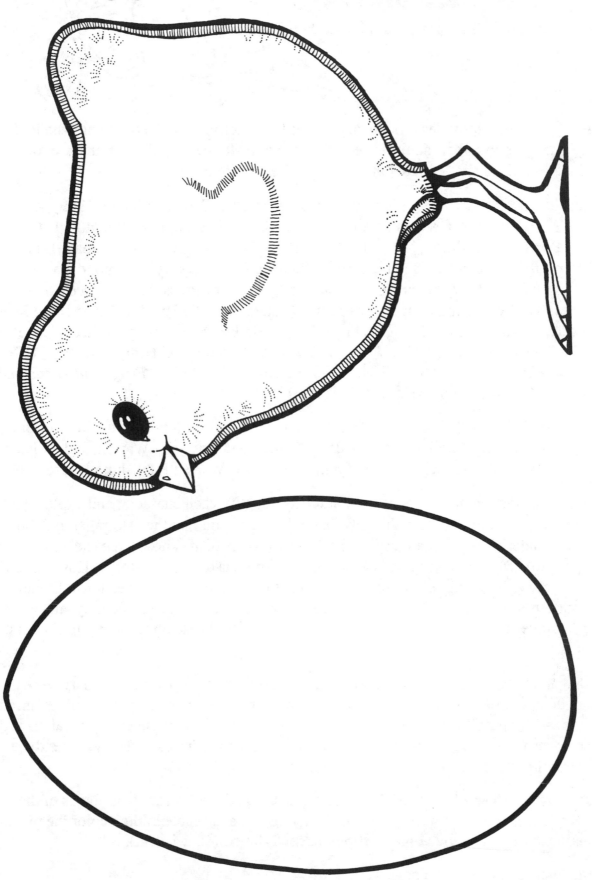

Life Cycles

Featured Literature: *The Caterpillar and the Polliwog*

Author: Jack Kent

Publisher: Simon & Schuster, 1982

Summary: This book provides a fictional account of a caterpillar and a polliwog who look forward to changing into their adult forms. With clever dialogue and illustrations, we follow the changes that take place and learn about two very different life cycles.

Additional Literature: *The Very Hungry Caterpillar* by Eric Carle (Philomel, 1969); *A Caterpillar's Wish* by First Graders of Alexander R. Shepherd School, Washington, D.C. (Willowisp Press, 1988); *Butterflies* by Elizabeth Elias Kaufman (Price Stern Sloan, 1986); *Look...a Butterfly* by David Cutts (Troll, 1982); *Bullfrog Grows Up* by Rosamond Dauer (Greenwillow, 1976); *What Is a Frog?* by Gene Darby (Benefit Press, 1957); *Insects and Crawly Creatures* by Dorling Kindersley Limited (Macmillan, 1992); *It's a Good Thing There Are Insects* by Allan Fowler (Children's Press, 1990); *Backyard Insects* by Millicent E. Selsam and Ronald Goor (Scholastic, 1981); *Frog and Toad* by Arnold Lobel (Harper & Row, 1976); *See How They Grow: Frog* by Kim Taylor (Dorling Kindersley, 1991); *Frogs and Toads and Tadpoles, Too* by Allan Fowler (Children's Press, 1992).

Related Songs: "Caterpillar Song" by Sandra Andert, "Flutter, Flutter, Butterfly" by Bonnie Woodard, "Growing Up" by Paula Schneider, "In the Pond" by Jean Warren, and "Listen to the Frog" by Susan M. Paprocki, *Animal Piggyback Songs* (Warren Publishing House, 1990).

Day 1: Introduce the featured book to your students. Identify each character and explain that the word "polliwog" means the same thing as "tadpole." Explain that the caterpillar and the polliwog will undergo major changes in the story. Do the students know what each character will change into? Do they think this is a factual book or a make-believe story? How can they tell? Read the story stopping to discuss the answers to your pre-reading questions. Explain that even though this story is make-believe, a caterpillar really changes into a butterfly, and a polliwog (tadpole) into a frog. Draw a simple Story Map for the Reading Center to show the main events.

Present the poem "Caterpillar and Tadpoles" on an overhead transparency or chart. Ask students to decide if the poem tells facts or if it is make-believe. How can they tell? Remind the children that a "tadpole" is the same thing as a "polliwog." Explain that a "chrysalis" is the shell-type covering a caterpillar spins around itself as it changes into a butterfly. Reread the poem several times, encouraging children to join in.

Reproduce pages 126 and 127 to use in making Life Cycle Strips to show the stages of the butterfly's and frog's growth and change. Completing one at a time, children color the pictures, cut out the boxes and then glue onto a strip of paper 24" x 6" (60 x 15 cm).

Send home the Parent Letter on page 120.

Life Cycles *(cont.)*

Day 2: Reread *The Caterpillar and the Polliwog*. Have students refer to the Story Map as a reminder of what happened in the story, and encourage children to create their own story maps.

Reread the poem, ''Caterpillars and Tadpoles,'' with your students several times, until they begin to participate.

Assemble and use little books of the poem by reproducing pages 122-125 and following the directions on page 4.

If you can find caterpillars and tadpoles in your area, collect and keep some in the classroom Science Center so children can watch their growth processes. Commercially-prepared kits with complete instructions are available:

Butterfly Garden	*Frog Hatchery Kit*
Insect Lore	Nasco
P.O. Box 1535	P.O. Box 901
Schafter, CA 93263	Fort Atkinson, WI 53538-0901
1 (800) 548-3284	1 (800) 558-9595

Explain that the class will watch real caterpillars and tadpoles for several days to see how they grow and change. Mention that there is always a chance the experiment will not work as planned. Let the class know the animals will eventually be released so they can take their natural place in the world.

For a fun art project, use egg carton sections to create your own caterpillars and tadpoles. Cut egg cartons in half lengthwise to obtain six connected sections to decorate with crayons or markers for caterpillars; add two-inch (5 cm) pipe cleaners for antennae. Decorate one egg carton section with crayons or markers for a tadpole's body; add a wiggly tissue-paper tail. After children complete their art projects, reread the poem ''Caterpillars and Tadpoles'' and have the children use their own caterpillars and tadpoles to dramatize it. House these egg carton pets at the science center during your unit.

Life Cycles (cont.)

Day 3: Begin by sharing some of the additional literature. Read the classic tale, *The Very Hungry Caterpillar*. Have children determine if this story is factual or make-believe. For more activities to do with this book, see *Connecting Science and Literature* (Teacher Created Materials # 341). Introduce The Caterpillar Counting Game (pages 128-130) and add it to the Math Center.

Begin reading one of the classic *Frog and Toad* books to your class. Can children tell if this book is factual or make-believe? How?

A Caterpillar's Wish and *Bullfrog Grows Up* are also enjoyable stories for young children. Are these stories real or make-believe?

Reread the poem, "Caterpillars and Tadpoles," while children play with their egg carton creatures.

Check on the progress of your caterpillars and tadpoles at the Science Center. Have children record their observations in a Science Journal (see page 144).

Day 4: Reread *The Caterpillar and the Polliwog*. Explain that butterflies are part of the very large family called "Insects" and frogs belong to the "Amphibian" family. Introduce the children to informational books about butterflies and frogs. Let the children know that the books you read next will be factual books that give true information; it is important for young children to understand that some books provide make-believe stories for us to enjoy, while others give us facts and information to help us learn.

Look...a Butterfly, *It's A Good Thing There Are Insects*, *Butterflies*, and *Insects and Crawly Creatures* are especially good books for young students, as they have simple text and wonderful photographs/illustrations. *Backyard Insects* has more text and good photographs, plus it challenges students to find insects in their own backyards. *Frog* and *Frogs and Toads and Tadpoles, Too*, both have simple text and wonderful photographs. *What Is a Frog?* has an abundance of information and helpful illustrations. After reading several books, ask students to help you make a list of insects on a large sheet of chart paper for future reference at your Science Center. Reproduce page 131 for your students to use in identifying insects.

Day 5: As the culmination of this unit, plan a "Back to Nature Celebration." This is the day when you will say good-bye to your butterflies and frogs by releasing them into suitable environments. While outside observe other insects and animals. See how many different ones you can find. Enjoy a celebration of nature!

Have children use crayons to draw pictures showing where the butterflies and frogs will now live. Have them include a sentence telling about their drawings. Compile into a Class Book or display at your science center. While they work, reread some of the children's favorite literature selections and sing some of the related songs about caterpillars, tadpoles, butterflies, and frogs.

Life Cycles Centers

Reading Center: Have literature selections including the poem, available at this center. Have children use the class Story Map as a guide to create their own story maps for any literature selection.

Writing Center: Have children use factual books for reference to make booklets of insect pictures that include a label or one-sentence description.

Math Center: Cut up green pipe cleaners to make about 100 one-inch (2.54 cm) pieces. Bend one end of each pipe cleaner to resemble the foot on a caterpillar. Prepare index cards with appropriate caterpillar-building tasks. For example, put numbers on the cards and have students assemble a caterpillar with the matching number of segments. Give older students equation cards (1 + 2, 2 + 4, 3 - 1, 5 - 3) and have them create caterpillars to match. Have children play the Caterpillar Counting Game (page 128-130).

Put plastic butterflies and plastic frogs (available from Oriental Trading, see address, page 56) into two separate estimating jars.

Science Center: Have children make daily observations of the caterpillars and tadpoles, and record changes with pictures in a science journal.

Encourage children to find insects and bring them in for a short time to be observed. Have several plastic magnifying glasses or Bug Observation Jars handy.

Maintain a good selection of informational books and posters about the topic. Encourage children to share about personal experiences with other animals' transformations.

Dramatic Play Center: Encourage children to use clothing and other items from this center to dramatize how a caterpillar makes a chrysalis and becomes a butterfly, and how a tadpole loses its tail, grows legs, and becomes a frog.

Art Center: Discuss the symmetrical design of butterflies. Then try making butterflies in one of these ways: (1) Use a clothespin for the body of the butterfly. Attach black strips for antennae and add eyes. Then scrunch the centers of two pieces of colorful tissue paper (about 4" x 6"/10 x 15 cm) into the clothespin to make the wings. (2) Fold a piece of bright construction paper in half. Have a template of a butterfly wing for children to trace. Cut out the shape and open it. Put small blobs of different colors of tempera paint on one side of the paper. Fold it shut and press down hard. Open up the butterfly, and you'll find a symmetrical design. Add eyes, body, and antennae with black scraps.

Parent Letter

Dear Parents,

We are currently working on an exciting thematic unit called "Life Cycles." We will observe real caterpillars and tadpoles as they grow and change into butterflies and frogs.

During our unit, we will enjoy several good books, both make-believe and informational, about butterflies, insects, and frogs: *The Caterpillar and the Polliwog* by Jack Kent, *The Very Hungry Caterpillar* by Eric Carle, *Backyard Insects* by Millicent E. Selsam, and *See How They Grow: Frog* by Kim Taylor.

Our activities about caterpillars and tadpoles will extend across the curriculum into science, reading, math, writing, art, and music. Plan to discuss with your child what we learn each day to reinforce the learning. Your child will bring home a little book of a poem, "Caterpillar and Tadpoles," to read with you. We've planned several interesting activities:

1. Making Life Cycle Strips to show the stages a caterpillar and a tadpole go through before becoming a butterfly and a frog.
2. Creating artistic caterpillars and tadpoles.
3. Making a list of insects.

Encourage your child's interest in butterflies, other insects, and frogs by taking them on a walk to find these animals in their natural homes. Please have your child draw a picture of a butterfly, caterpillar, insect, tadpole or frog that you find on your walk; then return it to school so your child can show it to the class. (Please label the animal with the label at the bottom of the page.) You might consider making a simple "bug jar" using a clear plastic jar with holes punched in the lid for your child to use in observing insects for awhile. Then return the insects to their homes in nature.

Thank you for your help and cooperation with our "life cycles" unit!

Sincerely,

This is a _____

Caterpillars and Tadpoles

Living things all change and grow.

Caterpillars and tadpoles do, you know.

Little caterpillars hatch from eggs.

Baby tadpoles hatch from eggs.

Caterpillars crawl as they grow strong.

Tadpoles grow as they swim along.

Caterpillars' legs will disappear.

Tadpoles sprout legs within a year.

Caterpillar becomes a butterfly.

Tadpole is soon a frog. Oh my!

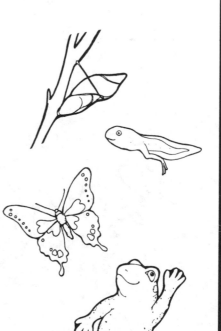

Butterfly learns to flutter and fly.

Froggie learns how to hop so high.

Living things all change and grow.

Frogs and butterflies did, you know.

Making Little Books

- -

My Little Book of

Caterpillars and Tadpoles

Name _____

- -

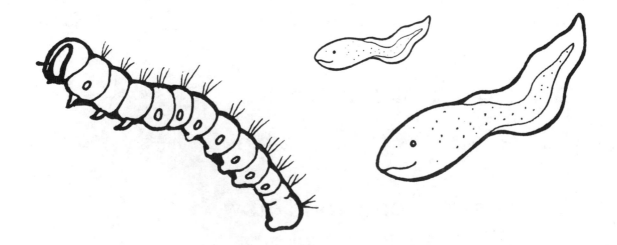

Living things all change and grow.

Caterpillars and tadpoles do, you know.

1

- -

Making Little Books *(cont.)*

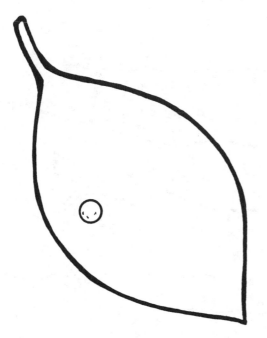

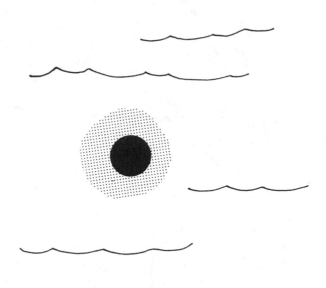

Little caterpillars hatch from eggs.

Baby tadpoles hatch from eggs.

2

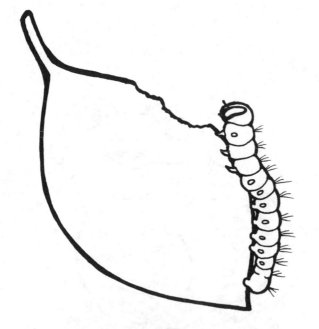

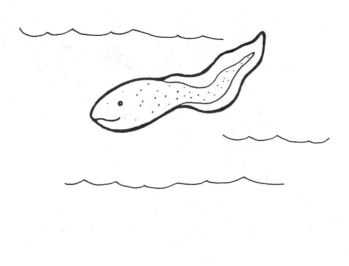

Caterpillars crawl as they grow strong.

Tadpoles grow as they swim along.

3

Making Little Books *(cont.)*

Caterpillars' legs will disappear.

Tadpoles sprout legs within a year.

4

Caterpillar becomes a butterfly.

Tadpole is soon a frog. Oh my!

5

Making Little Books *(cont.)*

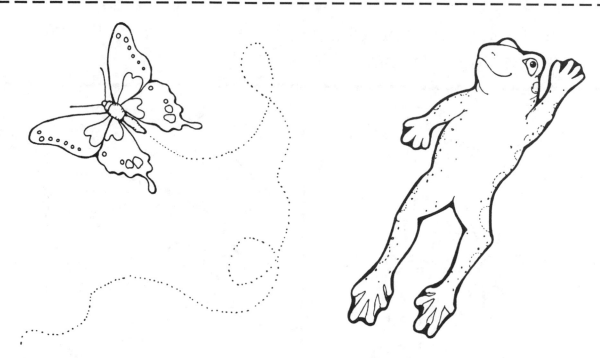

Butterfly learns to flutter and fly.

Froggie learns how to hop so high.

6

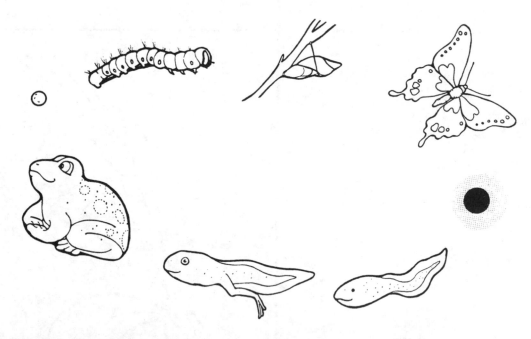

Living things all change and grow.

Frogs and butterflies did, you know.

7

Life Cycle of a Butterfly

Directions: Color, cut, and glue on 24" x 6" (60 cm x 15 cm) strip in the correct sequence.

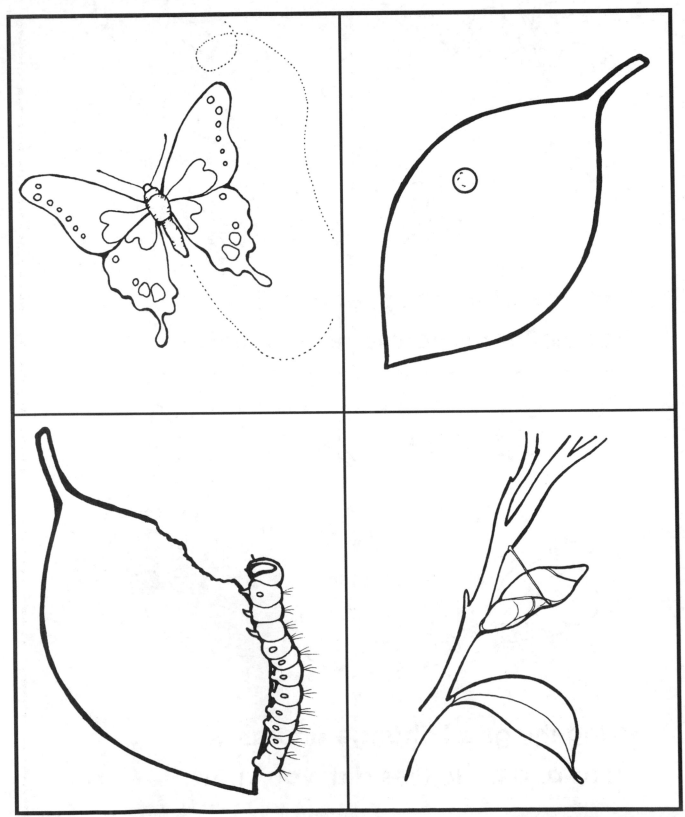

Life Cycle of a Frog

Directions: Color, cut, and glue on a 24" x 6" (60 cm x 15 cm) strip in the correct sequence.

Caterpillar

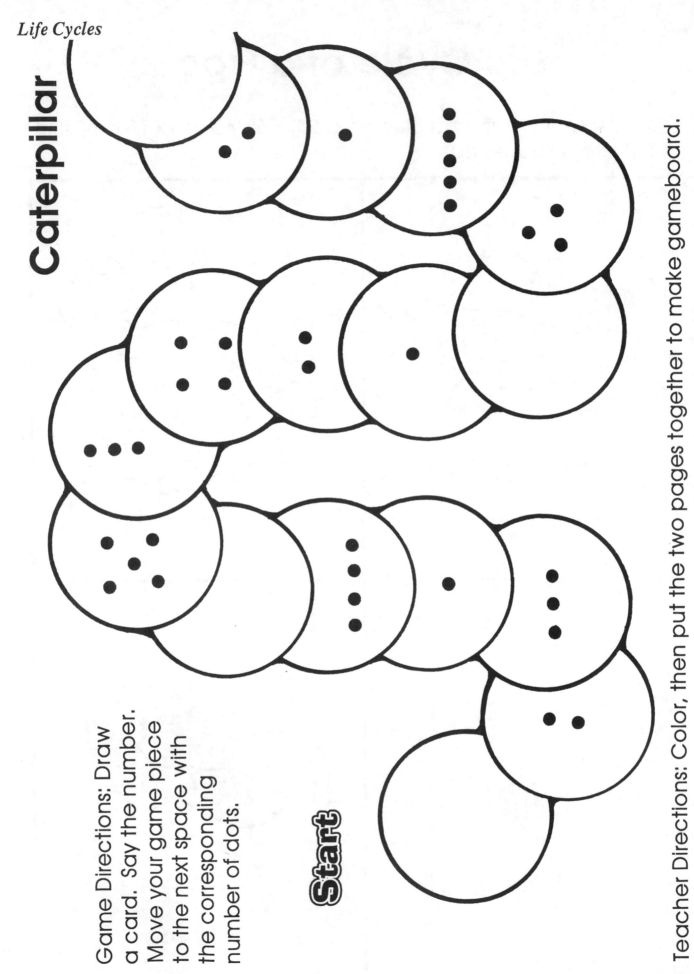

Game Directions: Draw a card. Say the number. Move your game piece to the next space with the corresponding number of dots.

Start

Teacher Directions: Color, then put the two pages together to make gameboard.

Finish

Counter Cards

Counting Gameboard

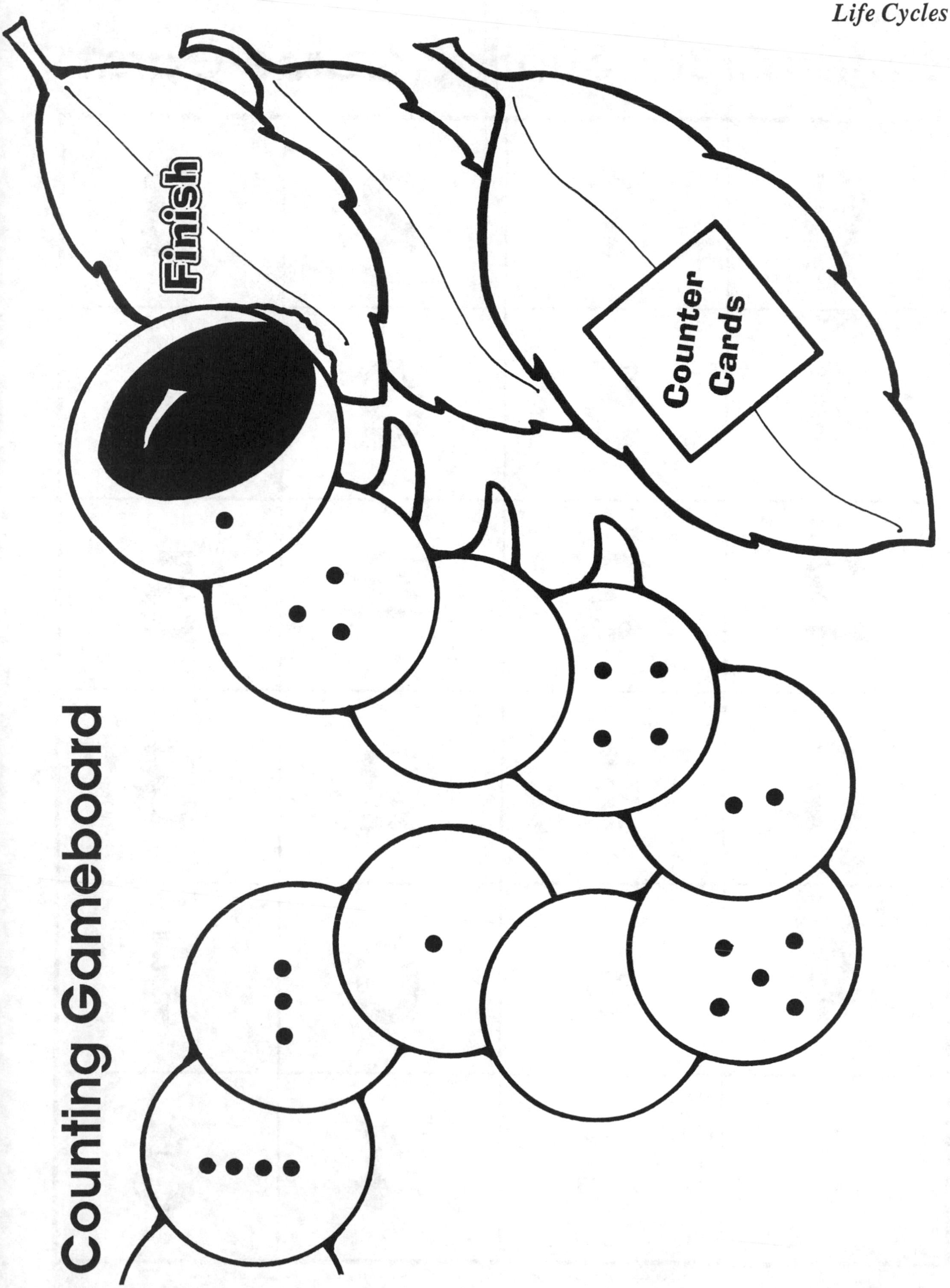

Caterpillar Counting Game Cards

0	1	2	3
4	5	0	1
2	3	4	5
0	1	2	3
4	5	0	1
2	3	4	5

Which Are Insects?

Directions: Decide which pictures show insects. Color the insects, then cut them out and glue them onto the grid.

These are insects.

Rocks

Featured Literature: *Rocks in My Pocket*

Authors: Marc Harshman and Bonnie Collins

Publisher: Cobblehill Books, Dutton, 1991

Summary: This story, about the Woods family, tells how useful rocks are. The Woods's use rocks to keep from blowing away on windy days, for games, and even for keeping warm. Something interesting happens when some city folks start buying rocks from the family and learn a good lesson about being honest.

Additional Literature: *Rock Collecting* by Roma Gans (Harper & Row, 1984); *Everybody Needs a Rock* by Byrd Baylor (Scribner, 1974); *Understanding and Collecting Rocks and Fossils* (Usborne, 1983); *Stone Soup* by Marcia Brown (Scribner, 1975); *Fossils Tell of Long Ago* by Aliki (Harper & Row, 1981); *The Magic School Bus Inside the Earth* by Joanna Cole (Scholastic, 1987); *Rocks, Rocks Big and Small* by Joanne Barken (Silver Press, 1990).

Related Songs: ''Old Volcano'' by Linda Warren, *Piggyback Songs* (Warren Publishing House, 1983); ''A Rock Song'' by Debbie Cerbus (Teacher Created Materials, 1993).

Day 1: Do a K-W-L activity about rocks (what we know, want to know, have learned). Make three large rock shapes out of brown or gray tagboard and write the three captions at the top; laminate. Ask what children know about rocks; write answers with wipe-off marker on the first rock shape. Accept all answers and put a question mark by those which must be verified.

On another rock shape, list what the children want to know about rocks. Put the rock shapes up in the room for easy referral. Add new questions to first shape; check-off questions as they are answered. Introduce the featured literature for the "rocks" theme. Ask class what rocks can be used for. As the story is read, check to see if any of your predictions appeared in the book.

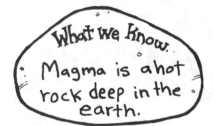

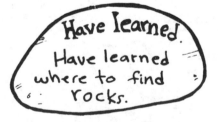

Ask the children for comments on the illustrations which resemble comic strip or cartoon drawings. After reading the story, have the children draw their favorite part of the story and add a descriptive sentence in invented spelling or dictated to an adult. Read the ''Rocks'' poem, or sing "A Rock Song" (page 141) to finish today's activities. Review songs and the poem throughout the week.

Send home the parent letter found on page 136.

Rocks *(cont.)*

Day 2: Ask if the children know what a collection is. Explain that people collect various things as a hobby and that some people collect rocks. Read *Rock Collecting* and show the children a labeled rock collection if one is available at your school. List on the chalkboard or a piece of chart paper some of the important vocabulary covered in the book (igneous, sedimentary, metamorphic) and other words which relate to rocks (stones, pebbles, boulders, gravel). Even though young children may not completely understand the harder vocabulary, this book does explain complex information in a very easy way.

Go on a rock-collecting field trip and become "rock hounds." If possible, collect rocks on school grounds or in the neighborhood. Children will also bring in special rocks from home (see parent letter, page 136). Have children classify individual collection into groups; eventually, have them choose their twelve favorite rocks to store in an egg carton. Decorate and label the egg carton with the students' names (e.g., "Christina's Rock Collection"). Read *Rocks, Rocks Big and Small.*

Day 3: Look back at *Rocks In My Pockets* and review the ways rocks were used. Talk about how people use rocks, such as building walls, making gravel, adding to rock collections, or in a game as in the story.

Invite a parent or guest to come in and share the hobby of rock collecting with your class. Try to bring in some of the special equipment a rock collector might use, such as a rock tumbler. Compare polished and unpolished rocks and talk about precious stones used in jewelry.

Teach the children games in which rocks are used for fun. One traditional game is a guessing game where a rock is hidden in one hand of one person and the other person must guess where it is. It's fun to keep a tally of the correct guesses as you play. Use rocks as markers for playing hopscotch; explain that rocks (chalk) are used for drawing the hopscotch grid.

Have the children color, cut, and assemble the little book about Rocks. Use as directed on page 4. Also, review the rock songs learned earlier in the week.

Day 4: Introduce the new centers for this theme and read the little book again for practice. Take a look at the rocks the children brought from home. Mark each child's initials on his/her rock with a permanent marker. Then sort and classify the rocks and arrange them in order by size. Keep the rocks for use later in the art center.

Rocks *(cont.)*

Do some experiments with different types of rocks, and examine some of their unique characteristics: pumice, sandstone, talc, etc. Pumice is a volcanic rock, the only one that floats. It is available at most grocery stores. Have the children try to scratch the sandstone, the talc, then their own rock — first with their fingernail and then with a regular nail. The sandstone is somewhat soft and some sand particles will scrape off (hold the rock over a sheet of black paper). Talc is very soft and comes off easily. Talc is used in making talcum powder. For many more ideas on experimenting with rocks, see *Rocks & Soil* (Teacher Created Materials #265).

For today's story read *Sylvester and the Magic Pebble*. Ask the children if they make wishes when they blow out their birthday candles or throw pennies into a wishing well. Tell them that the story is about wishes. What do they think Sylvester might wish for? How do they know the story is make-believe? After the story, give each child a small pebble which is painted red like Sylvester's magic pebble. Cut rock shapes out of white or manila construction paper. Have the children draw or paint what they would wish for with their pebble. Add a sentence to the picture: "If I had a magic pebble, I would wish for _____." Glue pebbles on the picture with craft glue or a hot glue gun.

Then cut some larger rock shapes in black, gray, or brown. Have the children sponge paint with a variety of colors on the large rock shapes to create the appearance of texture. The smaller rock shape with the children's pictures is then attached to the larger shape. Make sure a large portion of the sponge-painted rock is visible for the best effect. Display rocks on a bulletin board or assemble into a class book with a sponge painted cover. Do sponge painting at the art center.

Day 5: The last literature selection for this theme is *The Magic School Bus Inside the Earth*. Prior to reading the story, ask the children to predict what they might see inside the earth. Another good story is *Fossils Tell of Long Ago* which provides information relating to the fossil activity at the science center (see page 135).

As a culminating activity, have a rock exhibit or show. Have students practice, with a partner, describing the rocks in their egg carton collection: which rock is the shiniest? smoothest? prettiest? heaviest? favorite? Why? Invite parents or children from other classrooms to visit your exhibit. Have children wear their rock hound headbands (a center activity).

Finally, go back to your K-W-L charts from the first day. Make corrections as needed, make sure all questions were answered, and list new information the class learned on the third rock shape.

Rock Centers

Reading Center: Have plenty of books about rocks available, including multiple copies of the little book about rocks.

Have the children cut pictures that begin with "R," for "rock," out of magazines. Glue onto rock shapes and put up in the reading center as a display. Have children use pebbles to form letters or even spell words. Since salt and sand are rocks, have them trace letters in salt or sand trays.

Writing Center: Have available a variety of paper and writing implements and encourage the children to write stories about their pet rocks made in the art center.

To make a class book each child dictates or writes a fact learned about rocks during the unit and draws a picture to go with it. Assemble the pages within a rock-shaped cover.

Math Center: In the math center, have children work with measuring and weighing using non-standard rock (chalk) units. Provide some pieces of dustless chalk and some items to measure. Children set pieces of chalk along the edges of objects to determine their lengths in pieces of chalk.

Collect rocks of different sizes and weights. On a balancing scale, have children compare the weights of the rocks. If you have a sand table, the children can also work with containers measuring volume.

Have two estimating jars in the math center, one filled with pebbles and one with pieces of colored chalk. After all the estimates are written, count the items, grouping by tens and ones.

Science Center: Display the children's rock collections. This center should contain the materials and the directions for creating ''fossils'' (an adult helper will be required). Start a crystal garden and have the children observe the growth each day. Instructions for making fossils and crystal gardens can be found on page 143).

Art Center: Have children create a pet rock with the rock brought from home. Give the children an assortment of art materials to work with including yarn, trim, lace, plastic eyes, scraps of material and construction paper, and markers or paint. The rock can be transformed into a person, an animal, or an imaginary character. Use craft glue to attach materials to the rocks.

Sponge painting may be done by three or four children at a time.

Dramatic Play Center: After the pet rocks are completed, houses can be built for them. Challenge the children to try different types of blocks and other materials. After the houses are completed, measure them.

Parent Letter

Dear Parents,

In our new science unit, we will learn all about rocks: how rocks are used, what kinds of rocks people collect, and what the characteristics of some rocks — such as pumice, sandstone, and talc — are. If you have a rock collection you are willing to share with us, please send a note with your child within the next several days.

Our featured literature selection for this unit is *Rocks in My Pockets* by Marc Harshman and Bonnie Collins, a story about a unique family who finds many ways to use rocks. We will also read several informational books about rocks including *Rock Collecting* by Roma Gans.

We hope you enjoy reading the little book about rocks that your child brings home to share with you.

Our activities include many areas of our curriculum: writing, reading, math, art, music, and science.

Here are some of our planned activities:

1. Collecting rocks and sort by size, shape, and color.
2. Finding out how rocks are used.
3. Counting and grouping rocks by tens and ones and estimate how many rocks are in a jar.

Please help your child find a rock to bring to school. We'll use the rock in many of our learning experiences — and then we'll turn it into a Pet Rock to take home! The directions for this home assignment are listed below. Send in the rock by _____. Thank you for your help and cooperation with our activities.

Sincerely,

Rock Homework

Please use this "rock ruler" to help your child find a rock which is bigger than 1" (2.5 cm), but smaller than 4" (10 cm). The rock is due back at school by _____.

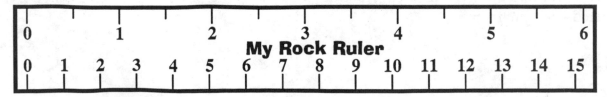

My Rock Ruler

Rocks

Rocks are everywhere I go —
They're always close to me.

Rocks are in a mountain brook,
And rocks are in the sea.

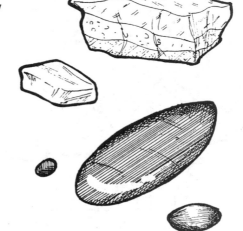

Rocks along a country road,
And in the desert sand.

Rocks are found in city streets,
And all across the land.

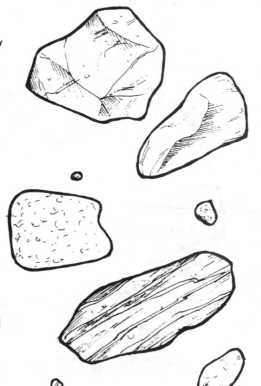

Small rocks, giant rocks,
Special rocks so rare —

All around our great big earth
Rocks are everywhere!

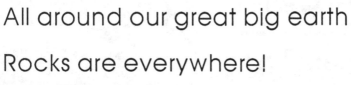

Making Little Books

My Little Book of

Rocks

Name _____

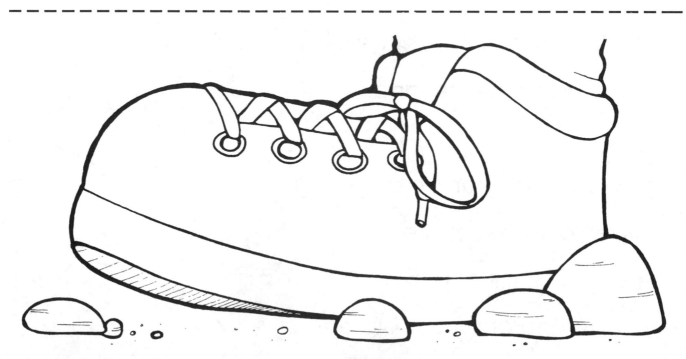

Rocks are everywhere I go —
They're always close to me.

1

Making Little Books *(cont.)*

Rocks are in a mountain brook,

And rocks are in the sea.

2

Rocks along a country road,

And in the desert sand.

3

Making Little Books *(cont.)*

Rocks are found in city streets,

And all across the land.

4

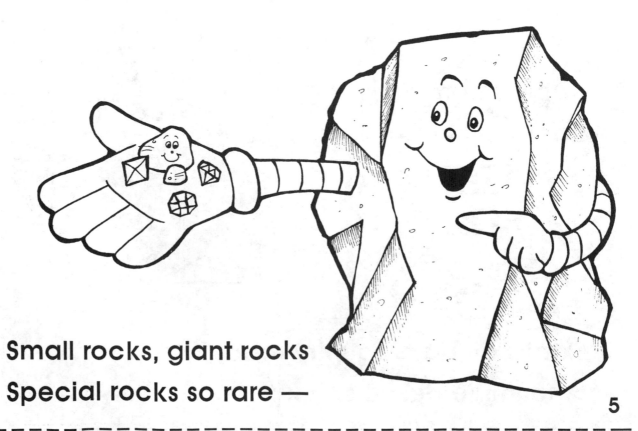

Small rocks, giant rocks

Special rocks so rare —

5

Making Little Books *(cont.)*

All around our great big earth

Rocks are everywhere!

6

"A Rock Song"

(Sung to the tune of *Frere Jacque*)

Rocks in my pockets,

Rocks in my pockets,

Big and small,

Big and small.

Shiny little pebbles,

Shiny little pebbles,

Found them all,

Found them all.

7

Rock Hound Headband

Color, cut, and attach the pattern below to a 2" x 24" (5 cm x 60 cm) piece of construction paper to make a headband. Adjust to fit.

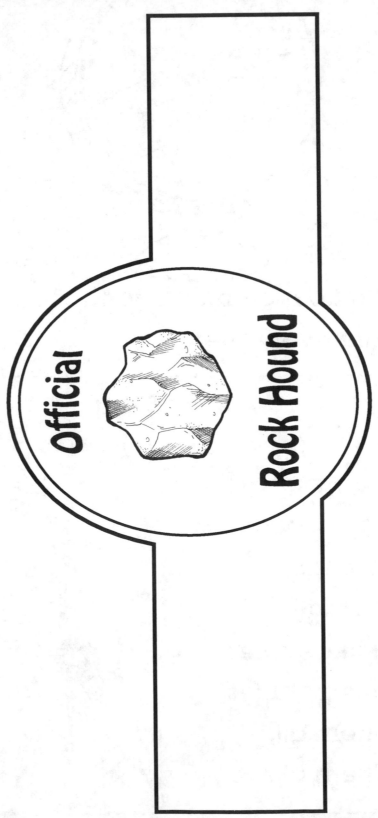

Rocky Science Activities

Crystal Garden

Make a crystal garden. Put charcoal in a disposable plastic bowl. Mix a solution of ½ cup (125 mL) liquid bluing, ½ cup (125 mL) salt, ½ cup (125 mL) water, and 1 cup (250 mL) ammonia. Pour it over the charcoal. (You can add a few drops of food coloring too.) Watch over several days. Record your observations in a Science Journal (see page 144).

Create a Fossil!

Provide each student with the following supplies:

1 ½ pint (700 mL) milk carton cleaned and dried (cut top section off)

1 bar modeling clay

A choice of "fossil" items (shell, leaves, bones, etc.)

    A. Have students press their clay into the bottom of their cartons and smooth out the top of the clay.

    B. Press the chosen "fossil item" firmly into the clay; remove.

    C. Prepare a mixture of plaster of Paris and pour a layer of plaster over each student's impression until it is completely covered. Set aside to dry.

    D. Tear the milk carton away from the clay and plaster. Separate the plaster from the clay. You now have a fossil!

Note: This type of fossil is called a "positive fossil." To create a "negative fossil," grease the top of the positive fossil with petroleum jelly and place in a second prepared milk carton. Pour a second layer of the plaster of Paris mixture over the positive fossil until it is completely covered. Set aside to dry. Remove carton and separate the fossil. Now you have two different kinds of fossils!

MY SCIENCE JOURNAL

Junior Scientist's Name: _____

Here is a picture of what I saw.